THE GOD WHO SOMETIMES SCREWED UP

IAN LAWTON

Rational Spirituality Press RSP

First published in 2018 by Rational Spirituality Press.
All enquiries to be directed to www.rspress.org.

A CIP catalogue record for this title is available from the British Library.

ISBN 978-0-9928163-4-6

Cover design by Ian Lawton.
Cover drawing by Artdzstock, licensed by dreamstime.com.
Author photograph by Simon Howson-Green.

a time to act

I am sitting in a cafe in the seaside town of Swanage, on the beautiful Isle of Purbeck, which forms the eastern edge of the Jurassic Coast world heritage site in southern England. I have lived here off and on for several years, but my good friends Stephen and Margaret are new arrivals. We have had a cooling swim on a roasting late-June day, and still none of us can quite believe how lucky we are to live in such an idyllic place. The conversation turns to my writing.

I have been researching spiritual books for longer than I care to remember. But in recent years it's become harder and harder to compete in a massively overcrowded mind-body-spirit market, where even the big names sometimes struggle. Despite still believing strongly in the power and uniqueness of my research and ideas, poor sales mean that increasingly I have to take long breaks to recharge my batteries – to wind myself up to yet again undertake the thousands of hours of painstaking research that characterises my more scholarly books.

That is really not meant to sound arrogant. It is just a plain fact that it takes a certain mindset and huge dedication to collate evidence from all sorts of places, and to try to pull it all together with as much skill as possible to form a coherent picture. My particular focus is on who we really are as spiritual rather than just human beings, and on the ground rules that govern our time in this earthly existence – and beyond.

Does that sound a bit over the top, or maybe even off-putting – too serious a topic for the ordinary person on the street? Well, look at it this way. Whatever kind of life you lead, or want to lead, isn't it worth putting just a little thought into trying to work out ‘how life works’? By that I don’t necessarily mean answering the big theoretical questions such as ‘why am I here?’ Instead I mean more practical questions.

For example, when things are good can I take the credit or is it just blind luck? Can I make it last, or am I expecting the proverbial to hit the fan at any moment? When it does, can I blame someone or something called God, or karma, or everyone around me? Do I go into victim mode, or do I just shrug and say ‘shit happens’ and wait for the good times to come back. Or do I try to work as hard as I can to *make* them come back? How much do I believe that I'm in charge of my life – if at all?

I know we're all supposed to be super busy these days, but can there be any human being alive who doesn't ask themselves questions like this at least occasionally? They matter, to us all. They are part of the human condition. Some would say part of the wonderful *mystery* of being alive, meaning they're questions that can't be answered. But I'm afraid I don't buy that – which is why I've been on the hunt for answers for nearly two decades. Some seekers join spiritual or religious movements, or devote themselves to meditation, or follow various gurus, sometimes travelling the globe searching for answers. Instead I've been drawn to work with evidence. Very, very good, and very, very consistent evidence. Of which more later.

Back to the conversation in the cafe. My friends know that several years ago I started researching a book called *Afterlife*. My thinking is that if I can definitively prove there is one, and describe what it's going to be like, that should be pretty interesting, right? Pretty universal? Especially if it turns out that down the ages we've been given a somewhat distorted idea of what to expect. But there's a problem. It is an incredibly hard book to research. So much source material, and so difficult to pull together and present as a logical whole.

At the beginning I worked hard on it for about six months. But then my spirits waned at the thought I might just be wasting my time putting *so* much effort into a book that only a handful of people might ever read. So about eighteen months ago I stopped and just concentrated on my 'normal' work that pays the bills – which is running training courses to teach people how to manage projects.

But simultaneously I escaped into my parallel world of fast bikes, racing cars, drinking too much beer and all the other distractions I use when trying to mask the nagging unfulfilment that your life's work, the thing you really care about most, is on hold and may never really take off. I am hardly alone in trying to plaster over the cracks when it all gets too much, am I? Especially when you've already spent way too long contemplating what might really be going on to produce such a frustrating and seemingly endless situation, and just want to kick back and relax for once.

But finally, in the last few months, I've come

back to the book with renewed vigour. In particular I've managed to finish off the part that deals with the less savoury aspects of the afterlife in what we might call the 'lower planes'. As you might imagine given the nature of the material this has been pretty distressing to research, but at the outset I promised myself that it would be dishonest, even pointless, to present a rose-tinted view that only delivered a partial map of the terrain.

So back to the cafe and my friends' question. I tell them that having finished this most difficult part of the book I'm taking a break again. After all it's mid-summer, the sea is inviting, the pubs are packed – and I've just bought a gorgeous American speedboat of the sort that appeared in the Bond movies of the late seventies. The only problem is it turns out to have not just one but *two* knackered engines, including the spare. But that's fine. It has already been worth the money just for the hilarity it's afforded my friends and family – and anyway there are still plenty of other distractions.

Stephen and Margaret understand my trials and tribulations. He has been editor of the world-renowned *Watkins Review*, or more recently

Mind Body Spirit Magazine, for many years. Every quarter he has to scan lists of a ridiculous number of new books to potentially review – literally several thousands – so he knows better than anyone just how much the market has become saturated with tomes of questionable quality, often just rehashing tired old ideas. He might be too diplomatic to say that, even after several glasses of Chardonnay, but I need have no such scruples and can tell it how it is. Meanwhile she has run a highly successful astrology-oriented publishing house for many years, as well as becoming an author herself more recently. They both understand the market far better than I do.

By way of contrast several years ago I wrote a simple book about the project management method I teach, which is called 'PRINCE2' – some of you will have heard of it, it's pretty well known. That book is selling at the rate of several hundred copies a month and, while I'm proud of it and grateful for the income it brings in, there's bound to be some frustration that my spiritual books are performing so poorly in comparison.

Sat around the table, we all agree that that's because the commercial book occupies an important niche for which there's obvious demand. Whereas when you're trying to put out a whole new brand of what I refer to as 'Supersoul Spirituality', it's very hard to reach people unless you're in a university environment, or already a big name, or manage to attract the backing of a major publishing house – and they're under huge financial pressures themselves, so less and less likely to take risks.

Stephen and Margaret are both convinced that I need to write about my personal experiences, but I'm reluctant. There is nothing extraordinary in my back story, certainly not from a spiritual perspective. I don't talk to or see spirits. I don't travel 'out of body', although I've tried. I am not an Eckhart Tolle, who found enlightenment living on a London park bench and has inspired millions with his wisdom. Nor am I a Neale Donald Walsch, who has apparently communicated with 'God' – or whoever the wise entity behind his communications might actually be.

No. I am just a normal guy who didn't show any trace of academic excellence when gaining a degree in economics, or when subsequently training as a chartered accountant. Although work-wise I've done many other things since then, still the most interesting thing about me is probably that I used to race bikes and cars with a bit of success, and that when I packed that in I replaced it with my writing and research. But it seems to me that none of this qualifies me to write a *spiritual* book about my own experiences. There simply aren't any worth writing about.

But my friends are nothing if not persistent. 'It's exactly the fact you're a normal bloke and just like anyone else that makes your spiritual journey interesting,' they insist. 'People have had enough of gurus they can't really identify with. They want to hear about the trials and tribulations of someone who still likes his bikes and cars, still likes to drink too much, talk rubbish and fall over occasionally, and still can't find true love even after decades of trying. That's *real*,' they chorus at me, 'that's what *real* people want now... someone who struggles with life sometimes, just like them!'

I can see their point, but I remain unconvinced.

Until Margaret hits me with the clincher. The

conversation has turned to social media, with which she's much more savvy than either of us guys, using it to promote her excellent debut novel about women suffering abuse. Now, one of the three fundamental planks of my spiritual worldview is the so-called 'law of attraction'. To put it simply the idea is that, however much it may appear that life is just happening *to* us, in fact each of us creates or attracts every single aspect of our life experience via our thoughts, beliefs, conditioning, expectations and so on.

The problem is that for some time now lots of best-selling books about this have been promising people the earth – that they can have literally *anything* they want simply by concentrating on it. While this is *theoretically* true, what most forget to mention or at least emphasise is that in practice most of us have a whole host of *subconscious* beliefs and programming – much of course stemming from childhood – which is often at odds with, and very effective at overpowering, our conscious desires. That is why as 'creators' we sometimes screw up. That is not to say there's any sense of right and wrong about this, merely that in some areas our lives may fall somewhat short of what we would ideally like.

Yet for me, to use this undoubted practical difficulty as an excuse to completely walk away from the basic truth of the law of attraction would be a huge and catastrophic mistake. In my recent books I stress that at the start of the twenty-first century humanity has finally started to glimpse the reality that each of us is a 'creator *god*' with unlimited power. That at long last we have the chance to leave behind our arguably childish superstitions about God, karma, blind chance – and every other excuse we've ever come up with to avoid taking full responsibility for the life each of us is creating. No more victimhood. What a huge and empowering transformation that promises for humanity!

So when Margaret reports that right across social media people have indeed been rejecting the law of attraction because they perceive that it just 'doesn't work', I need no more persuasion.

It will be difficult. It will be different from anything I've done before.

But I know I have to write this book.

1989

I come, I see, I conquer

'It'll take a bloody good rider to beat Bill today.'

My father Syd's face remains a mask of concentration, and shows no sign of humour or irony as he peruses the race programme. Various other family members are there but no one else even notices the comment. I don't know if he's trying to wind me up or is simply stating what he sees as a fact. After all he comes from tough, coal-mining stock in the Midlands, and is used to telling it how it is. But inwardly I seethe. 'I'll show you, you bastard.'

We are seated round the breakfast table in a hotel in Monza, just north of Milan. This will be the inaugural race for classic motorcycles on the historic track, home of the Italian Grand Prix ever since Formula 1 car racing began in 1950. Classic bikes of the type I ride were built before 1972, so they're relatively old and slow compared to modern machines, but the competition is still pretty fierce.

My nephew Mike is there. He is only fifteen but already well on the way to becoming one of my best friends. He tells everyone prepared to listen that Monza's straights are so long I have time to take a travel sweet from the glove compartment and read the paper before I get to the next corner. (For the overly literal, no, a bike *doesn't* have a glove compartment, but it's a joke, right?) Actually we still fly down them at more than 120mph, so we're not going *that* slow. You certainly know about it when at the end you brake and pull your head out from behind the screen that was keeping you as streamlined as possible. In years to come he'll become a pretty competent club racer himself and realise it's not quite as easy as it looks.

I am racing one of Syd's own bikes. Everyone has always called him Syd or 'the old man' for as long as I can remember, including us kids. It isn't a sign of disrespect, quite the opposite if anything. I have always seen him too as a best friend more than just a father, although I'm ashamed to report that I could be a proper *prima donna* sometimes when I was racing his bikes, and didn't always appreciate just how much he did for me.

Then again how would you like it if you'd been working hard all week in London and you got down to the family home in Southampton around 8pm on a Friday, hoping to load the bikes into your van and get away fairly quickly for what was often a journey of several hundred miles to whatever circuit we were racing at that weekend – only to find that he'd only just that moment started work on them and you weren't going to get away until the early hours? 'Oh pater, you really are a one!' doesn't quite cut it in that situation.

Syd had been a hugely successful motorcycle racer himself, starting before WW2 on home circuits and then, when hostilities ended, travelling all over Europe as part of what they used to call the 'continental circus'. The riders lived out of the back of their vans, prepared the bikes themselves, and earned just about enough in the way of start or prize money to get themselves to the next meeting.

As a 'privateer' he achieved enough decent results in international meetings and the odd Grand Prix that he attracted the attention of Joe Craig, the legendary manager of the Norton race team at the time. The British marque was the one to beat in those heady days before Italian then Japanese bikes came to dominate the sport. So he was offered his first 'works' ride in

1952 at the ripe old age of forty. Riders' careers could generally last longer in those days, plus he kept himself very fit, and of course he lost the war years when racing ceased for the duration.

He achieved plenty of wins and podium finishes in the Junior 350cc and blue riband Senior 500cc classes during 1952, albeit that the team were so dominant that Grand Prix placings were often determined by team orders and not by speed on the day. So by the beginning of 1953 he was tipped for the top. The first important race of the year was the 'North West 200' in Northern Ireland. Syd won the big race on the works 500cc Norton at a canter, on the final circuit smashing the previous year's lap record by a full thirty seconds. A famous picture shows him coming across the finish line, which in those days was on a fast right-hand curve, deliberately sliding the bike to gain maximum speed through the corner.

This was the curtain raiser for the first Grand Prix of the year at the famous Isle of Man TT, so he was firm favourite to take both the Junior and Senior races. But in practice a team mate accidentally hit his rear wheel and, although they weren't travelling at high speed, he was thrown high in the air and landed back on the tarmac – leaving him with twenty-seven fractures and recuperating in hospital for nearly six months.

My ever-resourceful mother Beryl had to relocate herself and their five young children from Southampton to Douglas, find schools for them, and visit Syd every day and try to keep his spirits up. She was some woman. My four eldest siblings, John, Pam, Barry and Christine in that order, were all born within around four years of each other. Imagine looking after that lot when pregnant much of the time, with no washing machine and so on – and Barry, the naughty one, doing his best to put everyone else's hands through the mangle. Then there was a seven-year gap before my nearest sister Sheila was born, then another seven years before I arrived some six years after Syd's accident.

Returning to which he nearly lost his foot when gangrene set in, but the only permanent injury was a stiff neck and his smashed right elbow being permanently set in a bent position so he could perform tasks with both hands. His mind took somewhat longer to recover because his racing career was over – another bad blow to his elbow would have meant amputation – but in time he set up what by the mid-1960s became the largest motorcycle dealership in Southern England. Not only that but in order to pursue his true love he began preparing race bikes for other people to ride, gaining huge success in that same swinging decade. In fact he became as well known as a gifted tuner and sponsor as he'd been as a racer.

His British bikes – Nortons and Triumphs ridden by riders of the calibre of multiple world champion Phil Read – won the prestigious Thruxton 500-mile endurance race for five years running from 1962 to 1966 – one of the winning riders being my brother Barry, no mean competitor himself as a youngster. Syd's bikes beat the factory-entered equivalents on each occasion, a testament to his skill at preparing reliable as well as fast motorcycles – and to the patience and fair-mindedness of factory engineers who spent hours answering his never-ending questions on the phone, knowing that most likely he would then go and beat their own entry.

But the marque with which he would become most synonymous was the Italian Aermacchi.

The lightness and nimble handling of these single-cylinder, pushrod-engined machines often allowed them to make up for any deficiency in power, and he became their UK importer in 1963.

His riders won a string of 350cc British Championships in the remainder of that decade, culminating with the hugely talented Alan Barnett placing second to the great Giacomo Agostini's MV Agusta in the 1970 Junior TT – recording an incredible-for-the-time lap of 99.99 mph that was tantalisingly close to the magic 'ton' for a single-cylinder 350cc machine. This unofficial record would last for nearly two decades, despite improvements in machinery, tyres, fuel and in the circuit itself, and was again a huge testament to the rider, the machine and the man who prepared it.

Syd's bikes won the Junior races at the amateur Manx Grand Prix in the Isle of Man for the next few years, but eventually the all-conquering two-stroke Yamahas ended their competitive life. The bikes were mothballed until 'classic' racing was born in the early 1980s, when he brought them out of retirement, most notably for the great Richard Swallow to win the Classic

Junior race at the Manx Grand Prix for five years running from 1987 to 1991. In the second of those years he finally bettered Barnett's time, averaging in excess of 100mph not just for one lap but for the whole race.

These achievements may not sound like much to the average reader, but to motorcycle racing enthusiasts they're almost the stuff of legend. That is why I'm hugely proud of my father, a fact that will have already become quite clear. But to return to the matter in hand, despite the almost impossible task of trying to follow in his footsteps, I was determined to race myself.

He insisted I should try trials riding first. These are slow-speed, off-road events in which the skill is not to put your foot down in often horrendously difficult 'sections' comprising vertical drops and climbs, huge boulders, river beds and so on. I was truly hopeless, although not helped by the fact Syd had tuned a bike that was deliberately designed to go slowly so that it could achieve at least 70mph – which I was happily doing one sunny day on the M3 taking it back up to London when the piston seized in the barrel and locked the back wheel solid. I managed to whip the clutch in to free the motor and coasted to a halt, unsure whether my underwear had survived the scare.

But that was as nothing compared to my antics once I actually started competing. As I said I was awful. I couldn't seem to master going slowly. Having failed spectacularly to achieve anything apart from a broken machine and a bruised ego in club events around London – on one memorable occasion I single-handedly demolished a barbed-wire perimeter fence, forcing the landowner to cancel the rest of the trial – I brought the bike back to Hampshire to enter novice events that included riders as young as seven or eight.

I fared no better. I remember watching a young lad on a child's bike give the throttle a quick squirt so that he could drop from the bank of a stream down into the bed with the bike horizontal all the time. 'Great idea!' I thought, 'I'll copy him.' His squirt turned into me giving the bike a big handful and sailing serenely across the stream before embedding myself firmly in the opposite bank. It was time to cut my losses.

Around this time we attended a race meeting at our local circuit, the aforementioned Thruxton, where Syd, Barry and I were 'parading' – fast riding but not an actual race. They were on the only two Aermacchis we had at the time, so for my circuit debut I'd been somewhat inappropriately offered a ride on a friend's beautiful and hugely expensive AJS 7R machine. I was crestfallen when, attempting to push start it in the pits, I ran out of room, grabbed the front brake too hard and down it went, breaking the gearchange lever. The bike had had new brake linings fitted that were very fierce in the wet conditions, but that didn't make me feel much better. Happily a new lever was procured, but the bike also suffered from a low-revs misfire that I couldn't master, which meant my ride wasn't particularly enjoyable.

Come the second parade towards the end of the day, Syd and Barry decided not to ride, the circuit being by this time absolutely drenched. Then, at the last minute, my sister Christine made up her mind that Syd really ought to let me loose on his bike. He was understandably reluctant after my earlier performance, but she was having none of it. So all of a sudden I was climbing into his baggy old spare leathers for my first ride on an Aermacchi. And I was going to impress them all, wasn't I? After all I had ambitions to follow in his footsteps all the way to the Grand Prix!

For three or four laps I circulated at ridiculously high speed for the conditions – I'd ridden a road bike in the wet but this was totally different and I had no idea where the limits were. Syd's approach to racing was always described as 'shit or bust', whereas apparently Barry built up gradually, but for better or worse it seems I took after the old man. My glory at being so much quicker than everyone else was short lived. A nice smooth slide along the tarmac as the bike's tyres finally cried enough on a tight bend saw me running to pick it back up, wondering if I'd done any damage and hoping like mad that no one would have to know what had just happened. The fact that next time around I came past the pits after something of a delay and also considerably slower probably gave the game away, but you can't blame a chap for trying. In any case the adrenalin had properly kicked in and I was hooked. I wanted more.

So what on earth has all this got to do with

being a god who sometimes screws up? Well, it's very simple. In the modern world all top sports people employ a psychologist. Probably the best known in the UK is Steve Peters, whose advice saw British cyclists conquer the world in the noughties. He subsequently helped world snooker legend Ronnie O'Sullivan to overcome his demons and still the chatter of his 'inner chimp' – that restless, sometimes hyperactive voice we all have that keeps questioning whether we're good enough, and tries to get us to worry unnecessarily about things from the past or that might happen in the future. In sports like snooker and tennis it's the ability to put a bad shot behind you, and to stay in the moment and refocus on the next one, that makes a huge difference. How often have you heard commentators talking about the crucial importance of the *mental* fortitude of consistent winners?

But there's another aspect to this mental approach, which is now commonly recognised but wasn't talked about much back when I was racing. It is called *visualisation*. For me this just became an obvious way to focus my mind before a race. It started with me making notes on a map of any given circuit about where I was going to brake for each corner, where I was going to peel in to it, where I was going to make my apex, where I was going to be throttling back on again, where I would be changing gear, and so on and so forth. I guess as a fairly logical and organised guy I was just trying to take the randomness out of it and make it a repeatable process. Then as I got quicker when learning the different circuits, or because I was on a quicker bike, I would update my notes.

But this gradually developed into something more. I began to visualise being the first person away from the startline – in classic racing we still did push starts rather than having the engine already running. This wasn't too hard for me because I'm tall and have the leverage, and I could pretty much guarantee being first away unless I was right at the back of the grid. Then as I became more competitive and started winning I'd experiment with visualising perfect laps of the circuit, with as much detail as I could put in.

Finally and probably most important, once I started to compete for championships against specific rivals, I would visualise crossing the line ahead of them. I would also internally verbalise all the reasons why I was better than them and was going to beat them. I would go out running down the Thames tow path from my home in Fulham to Putney Bridge, and during the tough sprint finish I would be shouting – sometimes out loud – 'I'm better than you!' as I pictured my rival's face. It would be the same when doing press-ups on my fists, deliberately in the gravel by the side of the road so it would hurt more.

I hope that doesn't make me sound like a psycho! Some of these people were good mates – after all, I wasn't at that level where to have any sort of camaraderie would weaken my competitiveness. But for me it was all part of having a winning mentality.

Let us be clear, I still had to have a competitive bike, know the circuit fairly well and have a reasonable degree of talent. I certainly didn't feel I could just magic up winning out of thin air. But if all those things were equal between me and a rival, I would back myself to beat them by mental strength. I guess you could even call it arrogance, and in my case there probably was an element of that. But any sportsperson will tell you that you have to have a huge ego to be competitive. Some mask it well with genuine humility, but that desire to be the best will still be there under the surface.

The only exception to this rule is sportspeople who have *so* much more natural talent than their rivals that they can have huge doubts about themselves and still win. My understanding is that O'Sullivan was probably one of the finest ever examples of this, certainly before he worked with Peters.

Born in 1959, in common with so many households of my generation ours was at least nominally Christian, although I can't remember religion ever being discussed much. It was all bikes, bikes – and then more bikes. My poor mother.

At the age of thirteen I was sent away to Canford boarding school in Dorset and initially I was terribly bullied. With that seven-year margin to my nearest sister Sheila I led a pretty sheltered childhood – often reading for hours on my own in our large house in one of the most affluent suburbs of Southampton, where kids didn't play in the street. The peace was shattered by the arrival of a small Honda 'monkey bike' when I was around five and, after a slow start learning how to ride it, I'd spend every hour I could thrashing it around the garden.

This meant that Sunday mornings weren't very spiritual either. Instead of going to church the whole family, including the various partners of my elder siblings, would gather at home and take it in turns to do timed laps round the u-shaped front driveway, onto the pavement of the road outside – people were much more easy-going then, even though it was an affluent neighbourhood – and back round again. Five laps was the norm and I was convinced I'd set a new record one day only to find my sister Christine was so busy nattering she'd forgotten to click the stopwatch off. I was devastated. Then one day I came home to find Syd had sold the bike to a school friend without even telling me! I never did find out why, but I was bikeless for quite some time after that.

Our other Sunday morning ritual was for the whole family to go horse riding from a stables in Whiteparish. Sheila and I in particular used to enjoy this, and we both entered several gymkhanas. She was much better than me and a natural horsewoman but, given that I wasn't much good at other sports, I was delighted to win one of these events on one of the school's worst behaved horses. I was even presented with a beautiful crop all of my own, only for Sheila to steal it and maintain ever afterwards that she'd won it. Sisters eh? But in the end I got thrown from a horse so many times that I felt motorbikes, which didn't have a mind of their own, would be a lot safer.

Initially this didn't prove to be the case however. First of all there was a brief stint with a Yamaha motocrosser, which spent much of its time upside down in a field with me pinned underneath it. Then at age sixteen Syd bought me a black Fantic Caballero moped for the road, of which I was mightily proud. As always he tuned it to within an inch of its life, and a whole bunch of us used to tear around making real nuisances of ourselves. To be honest it was amazing no one got themselves killed with some of the stunts we used to pull.

But on one occasion I misjudged a downhill bend and went straight into the back of a parked car, although my injuries only extended to covering the inside of my jacket with Kentucky

Fried Chicken. On another I went up the back of a car at some traffic lights when he stopped suddenly on amber. Now my bike had a small map pouch on the tank, so no prize for guessing which part of my anatomy stopped me dead as I slid up into it at high speed. Not only did the impact leave me by the side of the road groaning and clutching my battered jewels, which didn't seem to elicit any sort of sympathy from the stern university lecturer whose car I'd hit, but I spent the next six months thinking I was impotent. Without going into details I woke up the next Christmas morning to the knowledge this wasn't the case, and it was the best present I've ever had.

Back to school. Because of my sheltered childhood I simply didn't develop the skills required to survive in the rough and tumble of a boarding environment, where the slightest weakness was prayed upon – at least in my time, it may have changed somewhat now. My parents knew I was unhappy, but I didn't dare tell them about the remorseless bullying because I knew at least my mother would insist I was removed. Something inside told me that I had to get through it, that it would make me a better and stronger person.

In hindsight I think that toughening up did do me good in one respect, because it prepared me for some of the challenges I've faced since and made me the man I am. Having said that I also respect the sensitive and loving child I once was. For example I have a very distinct memory of standing with my mother at a market stall selling shoes, and being devastated that a little girl of similar age who didn't have any was begging for a pair. I have no idea where her parents were and, being only four or five, I couldn't do anything to help. But I remember crying about that for a long time when I got home. So in another sense it seems a shame that that loving, empathetic little boy had to toughen up. Indeed I've been trying to bring that side of me back much more to the fore in recent decades.

As for religion, I did undertake 'confirmation', but in truth a major motivation was that we got a weekend away from school and some girls from another school would be there. I guess it was appropriate that I stood to receive the blessing rather than kneeling – my left knee having being immobilised in a rugby accident – because as my intellect developed in my later teens I increasingly refused to bow down to any notion of divinity.

Actually this was no great intellectual process – it was based much more on practical observations. Of the way in which most people only prayed when they were in deep trouble, or as part of a repetitive ritual that seemed to have no real meaning or relevance. Also of the fact that most of the really devout pupils at my school, the ones in the voluntary Christian fellowship group, unfortunately came across as the most weak and insecure among us. I should know because at one point – when lonely and in desperation after being on the receiving end of a bad period of bullying – I joined them, but found the atmosphere insufferable.

More than this, though, we had to sit through countless divinity lessons and sermons at school, and as soon as I started to really think for myself I realised that these left me cold. Without wishing to cause offence, from a purely theoretical perspective the basic tenets of Christianity seemed to me to be completely irrational. Of course I knew even then that throughout history thousands of people have shown immense courage and integrity in helping others or in defending their religious beliefs – whether Christian or otherwise – and none of my comments are intended to detract from their bravery and selflessness. But there have been plenty of others who have used religion as a cloak to attempt to control and subjugate their fellow man, and to garner power and prestige.

So it was that I became convinced that religion was for those who *needed* to believe because they were too feeble to exist without that vital crutch. I was convinced that real power and strength comes from within oneself, not from some external deity. I had found that out for myself, the hard way, by finally toughening up. I even became pretty popular amongst the schoolmates who had once tormented me, and ended up as head of house and deputy head of school.

This brought quite a few perks. For a start as school prefects we had our own common room where we could eat and drink to our hearts content, and generally chill out. Having said that, even though I wasn't brought up as a Catholic, can you imagine the guilt when you later find out that for several years you'd been throwing darts at a board mounted on a painted-over, long-lost, 3000 year-old Assyrian frieze from Nimrud? It turns out it had been brought back from Mesopotamia in the mid-nineteenth century by renowned archaeologist Sir Austen Henry Layard, who had a connection with the Guest family who then owned Canford Manor, and who had somehow just forgotten about it. You have got to be seriously wealthy to overlook something like that, but there you go.

Better still, after supper I could amble down to the bike sheds or any other place where the more junior members of the school used to congregate to smoke, tell them to bugger off fast or I'd punish them, then my companions and I could have the place to ourselves and smoke to our hearts' content. Come on, there had to be some abuses of power to make up for the extra duties and responsibilities.

All in all, then, when I finally left school I proudly trumpeted my atheism to anyone who would listen. I even looked up the word *agnostic* in the dictionary just to make sure, but no, I was definitely an *atheist*. What I didn't know then in my youthful arrogance, and what prominent atheists like Richard Dawkins still haven't understood, is that there's far more to this 'power from within' lark than meets the eye.

Of course I've been on something of a spiritual roller coaster since then, and almost everything in my outlook has changed. But for now it's a rather wonderful squaring of the circle that the sort of visualisation I was practising back in my racing days is intrinsic to using the law of attraction to consciously direct one's experience – and that, as I indicated in the first chapter, the law itself forms one of the fundamental planks of the supersoul model of spirituality I've more recently developed. It is, in fact, all about power from within. But it's not a material, earthly power that's being wielded, but rather a spiritual and energetic one.

So how effective was all this visualisation in my racing career? Well, after various further parades in the latter part of 1980, several of which again ended in tears, I began racing proper the following year. Results on Syd's small 250cc and larger 408cc Aermacchis were by no means spectacular to begin with, but by the middle of the following year I got my first win on the big bike at a former airfield circuit near

Keevil in Gloucestershire. In a close finish I outbraked two rivals into the last corner at the end of a very long straight, where my sister Pam happened to be watching. What is more I'm ashamed to say it's always given me a kind of perverse pleasure that she afterwards thanked me for making her so nervous she was sick by the side of the track. I guess it made me feel like a bit of a hero. Blasted ego again I'm afraid.

My brother Barry had made a comeback in classic racing several years before this, and was doing well, with plenty of wins under his belt. We weren't massively close back then because we're very different people, but now it's wonderful that we can enjoy reminiscing about several memorable races against each other on 350cc machines.

One was again at Thruxton where, knowing we would probably be first and second away from the start, Barry confidently told me to tuck in behind him so he could show me the line through the ultra-fast, sweeping bends round the back of the circuit. The plan worked until I could see him getting closer and closer to the outside of the track as we were laid over through one of the fastest curves, at which point

I thought, 'Sod it, I'm backing out of this one, he's going off!' – just as he suddenly lifted the bike upright and disappeared off into the cornfield on the outside of the circuit at high speed. Amazingly he managed to stay on and repassed me later in the race, finishing well up the field – I think he even maintains he won.

On another occasion at Snetterton in Norfolk we passed and repassed each other throughout the race. He did eventually win, with me second, but that was the last time he beat me. Although I'm sure it was completely coincidental, he retired not long afterwards.

I ended up winning a great many races on Syd's wonderfully prepared bikes over those first few years, including multiple wins in the prestigious 'Classic Races of the Year' also held at Snetterton, and several championships. One standing joke from this time is that, with race weekends often being quite a family affair, and with me tending to sweat fairly heavily while competing, whenever I came in mother would feel compelled to take a 'wet wipe' to my fevered brow. She also had special sandwiches in a container with my name on it, and woe betide anyone – mainly Barry – caught trying to steal them. I guess she was just trying to make up for all the bullying at school, or something, but these are things I'll never be allowed to live down.

My girlfriend during this period was Anna – the only daughter of the actor Gareth Thomas, who played the lead role in the sci-fi series 'Blake's 7'. The first time Syd met her she was removing his exceedingly heavy toolbox from my van with just one hand – exactly the sort of thing to guarantee his everlasting admiration. However we had an on-and-off relationship. I loved her enthusiasm for life, and her ability to drink pints of snakebite without apparent effect, but unfortunately she was very insecure.

We were together for some years, so in the end I thought if we got engaged it might allow her to feel more secure. Sadly it didn't, and if anything she got worse. Gareth and I were pretty close, we often used to drink and chat late into the small hours, so after she'd gone to bed one night I plucked up the courage to tell him I felt I'd have to call the engagement off. He simply laughed and said, 'I don't blame you, I couldn't deal with her either!' Poor Anna. I was saddened but not entirely surprised when Gareth's obituary reported that she'd predeceased him.

All that aside, my visualisation techniques were clearly working at the level of classic racing, but I was keen to move on to more modern machinery if I was going to fulfil my ambitions. So for the beginning of the 1984 season Syd got hold of a relatively dated TZ 350cc Yamaha so I could start competing in modern racing. Unfortunately it had a hard-to-trace carburetion problem that meant I was nearly always last away from the start.

I had some half decent results, including a few third places, but the bike was fairly slow – despite Syd's unstinting efforts to learn how to tune a two-stroke engine for the first time in his life, aged over seventy. I found out afterwards that for a time he was phoning one of the top two-stroke Grand Prix experts virtually every day trying to gain more insights. Most of the top four-stroke tuners of Syd's era doggedly refused to move with the times and learn entirely new skills, but Syd was no ordinary man.

In any case for the following year I built up a completely new bike from parts, using a more modern alloy frame with better suspension.

Most important Syd had persuaded an old pal, another well-known two-stroke tuner called Arnie Fletcher, to provide us with one of his LC Yamaha engines that were dominating the Formula 2 world championship at the time. It produced a highly competitive 78 bhp and I felt sure I could perform well with this machine.

We got the engine so late I had no time to practice before the first meeting at Snetterton, yet in a horribly wet opening race I won comfortably against much more powerful open-class machines. We were over the moon – but not for long. In the second I had to fight my way through from a poor grid position, and was up to third halfway around the first lap when I lost it. The bike was fine but as I got up I realised my shoulder felt strange: my first broken collarbone. It wasn't helped when Syd had to drive my VW van home and, in his excitement and with mixed emotions, tried to overtake a long line of stationary traffic – ploughing straight into the car at the front as it turned right.

My girlfriend at the time, Cheryl, had been propping me up against the back window to stop me from moving around too much, but now we were both thrown onto the floor of the van amongst various petrol cans and such. As was his way Syd tried to tough it out, but got fairly short shrift when he opened up the back door and sparked up a cigarette. I was taken by ambulance to Bury St Edmunds hospital, where I had to explain my collarbone had already been broken *before* the accident. Much more seriously Cheryl suffered internal bleeding and I sat with her all night in the critical ward, willing her to be ok. She was, but quite understandably Syd and I weren't exactly big favourites with her family from then on.

Two months later I was at Snetterton again, with me and the bike now repaired and raring to go. But again I was trying too hard and rode right over the edge of the tyres on the 100mph-plus Coram curve. I slid along the ground but the bike landed on top of me, breaking all the ribs on the left of my chest and puncturing a lung. With an oxygen mask on to help my breathing, the lovely St John's nurse who sat with me on the ambulance journey to Norwich hospital had to keep looking closely into my pupils to check I wasn't passing out. But the poor lady was so cross-eyed that at such close range each of her eyes was looking right over to my ear on the opposite side. Funny if I'd been in the mood to enjoy it, but instead I vowed during that bumpy and painful journey that, as long as I lived to just be able to go to the pub again with my friends, I would pack racing in. Of course within months I was back and winning on Syd's bikes.

The following year, 1986, I went to Snetterton yet again for an ACU Star meeting, my first step up into national rather than club racing – which meant using slick rather than treaded tyres for the first time. However I'd driven overnight from a wedding in Liverpool, and had no chance to fit the new tyres for practice. A number of friends travelled up from London to watch me in the first race on a baking hot day, but I told them not to expect anything great with no proper preparation and a higher level of competition.

To my surprise I got away in third place and no one came flying past me, although I did have a race-long dice with one other rival. His bike was slightly quicker but I could outbrake him, so on the final lap I eased past him at the end of the main straight, confident I could stay in front round the rest of the lap for a thrilling first national podium. But I was forgetting my jinx at Coram curve, and the fact I wasn't used to slicks.

As we rounded it for the final time, laid right over at high speed, I felt both tyres start to slide. The back sliding is fine, but when the front goes too it's a lot more scary. I did what I was always used to doing and what's instinctive – I backed off on the throttle. The trouble is when you do that with slick tyres the rear slows down and then grips again, immediately flicking the bike upright into a 'highside'. The bike actually carried on for several hundred yards before ploughing into a concrete marshal's post at high speed, which didn't do either a lot of good.

As for me, I did a passable impression of a low-flying aircraft before completely forgetting Syd's advice to roll up into a ball *and stay there*. You see, whenever you're sliding or flying along after an accident, the desire to stop as soon as possible, and particularly before you've hit anything, is understandably strong. The problem is you can convince yourself you're stationary when in fact you're still doing about 40mph. Anyway, I put an arm out way too soon and my hand was pushed very hard up into my forearm.

Now I'm always one for accepting that if you take risks you accept the consequences, and normally the St John's medical volunteers were brilliant. I thought by this time I knew all of them at Snetterton anyway. But on this occasion, as I sat resting against the Armco and thinking about how much my bloody hand hurt, I was suddenly engulfed in a huge black shadow. Looking up, the most enormous woman was standing over me. 'What's the matter with you then?' she asked in a voice several octaves lower than it had any right to be.

'I've hurt my hand a bit,' I replied, trying to sound as brave as possible, although in truth I was fairly heavily knocked about. She immediately bent down and made a grab for my gloved appendage. I hurled a colourful stream of expletives in her general direction as I snatched it away – although at least I refrained from suggesting that becoming intimate with a man at least once in her life might do her some good.

None of this was helped when my so-called friends turned up at the hospital. By this time my hand had been x-rayed, as well as my previously-broken collarbone – when I asked why they casually replied, 'Because we're going to need to kneel on your shoulder to pull your hand out of your arm.' Too much information I felt, but never mind. In any case, so there I was in a bed, thankfully in a room on my own, waiting to go into theatre with the usual 'Nil by Mouth' sign at the head of the bed, when in pranced my friends – led by then best mate Doug, the arch prankster of them all.

Remember it had been a boiling hot day, and I hadn't been allowed a drink ever since the accident. They brought me a Terry's Chocolate Orange. Better still they also brought me a pornographic magazine that had only men in it, propped it up on the bedside table open at the centrefold, and ran giggling out of the room and back to London – knowing I was too banged about to be able to easily reach over and knock it onto the floor, and calling the very attractive duty nurse in the process. I am not easily embarrassed, but I simply had no words to explain what was going on when she walked in. So for once I just lay there and said nothing.

Eventually I'd had enough of hurting myself on modern bikes and, though I was still happy to race Syd's classics, I turned to four wheels in my search for glory. But that's a whole other story.

So, back to Monza. I have never told Syd about

my visualisations, but I've been doing them that morning. Going through every bend, every gearchange, every braking point. I see myself vividly on the top step of the podium, looking down at Bill.

By the way the Bill in question is Bill Swallow, the brother of Richard who won so often in the Isle of Man for Syd. Not long afterwards Richard was tragically killed by his stepson in a horrific drug-induced attack, and not only were he and Syd a brilliant team but I thought of him as another brother. So many memories. Racing go-karts in an otherwise empty Onchan Stadium after one of his wins, which was only ever going to end in tears as each of us became increasingly desperate to beat the other. Going out for a few beers in London whenever he came down from Yorkshire for work. The faulty spark plug that Syd had used for more than twenty years 'because it had proved itself', but which finally gave up the ghost when Richard was in the lead of a race – and which he then launched about half a mile into an adjacent field. Him watching me after he broke down in the Pre-TT Classic races on the narrow, bumpy, seven-mile Billown circuit in the south of the Isle of Man, where in my first ever road race I managed to finish second to Bill, and Richard congratulated me on being 'bloody fast lad' on one of the trickiest parts of the circuit. All of these are very dear to me.

But actually Bill is probably the better known of the two brothers and also a terrific bloke, although I don't know him quite so well. He has been at the top of classic racing for many years, so it's a big thing for me to beat him. I will be up against him again in two weeks time on my second visit to the Pre-TT Classic, so I want to draw first blood. I have started racing cars now, but I'm still doing the odd bike race.

Actually I have another reason. My godfather was the late, great Bob McIntyre, a legendary Scottish racer who was great pals with Syd. One of my proudest possessions is a silver egg-and-spoon set he bought me for a christening present when he came all the way down to Southampton for the event, which shows the kind of man he was. I still ride with the spoon tucked into my right boot as a lucky charm. Unfortunately he was killed at Oulton Park in 1962 aged just 33, but not before he had set the first ever 100mph lap of the TT circuit on a works 500cc Gilera in 1957, and a new one-hour speed record of an astounding 141mph on a 350cc Gilera later that same year – on the incredibly bumpy, original, banked Monza circuit. He had a huge number of other successes on a variety of machinery, and was so popular that literally thousands of well-wishers turned up for his funeral to pay their last respects. My middle name is Robert, after him – and the Monza connection gives me another very good reason to win this afternoon.

But it's not going to plan. In first practice Bill and I have lapped at similar speeds while getting to know the circuit, but in the second session he has improved his time substantially while I haven't. Hence Syd's probably reasonable observation over breakfast.

In the race Bill and I tear off into the lead, and it's not long before we're about half a lap ahead of the rest of the field. Everyone assumes I'm on Syd's special 'short stroke' 350cc Aermacchi, but actually that motor has a problem so we're just using a standard engine. It is still pretty good on top speed, which is what you need round here. But lap after lap I'm trying to hang onto Bill, and each time around he's eking out just a bit more of a gap. I am doing all I can, but by the start of the last lap he's a good few hundred yards ahead as we cross the line. I know I'm going to need a miracle – and just then he gives it to me.

As he exits the first chicane he runs just a little wide, and while it's only a small mistake it forces him to momentarily feather the throttle instead of jamming it wide open. 'I've got you, you bastard!' and suddenly I'm gaining on him hand over fist. As we round the Curva Grande we're both laid over, tucked in behind our screens with throttles pinned to the stop. Finally I'm only inches from his rear wheel, benefiting from his slipstream.

I am ready. Maximum concentration. In the zone. One part of me knows it's probably madness to be doing this, another is exhilarated by the huge adrenalin rush. I dive out from behind him moments before we start to brake for the next left-right chicane. I choose the left hand side so I've got the dominant line into it and can push him wide if I have to. The slipstream effect takes me nearly alongside him and then I brake just fractionally later. I am ahead as we approach the corner.

Then disaster! I see a stationary yellow flag. Immediately I can see it's warning us of a bike parked up against the Armco barrier on the exit, but the flag's not being waved and it's not a serious hazard. You aren't supposed to overtake under even a stationary yellow, but neither of us was aware it was being shown until after I was alongside him. To have to brake harder now and drop back behind would be a travesty – besides which I'm on the braking limit, so I'm not sure I could even if I wanted to.

I fly through the chicane, then I'm absolutely on the edge. I will *not* let him back through again. I have no time to look back as I tear into the twin Lesmo corners, using all the road and a bit more, then down the short straight, under the bridge and into the fast, flowing, left-right-left at Ascari. I have never been through there so quick on any other lap, so much so that afterwards even Barry – watching there but not always the swiftest to praise his younger brother – says I was seriously fast on that last lap.

My head is jammed behind the screen on the penultimate straight, everything tucked in to be as streamlined as possible. I dare not waste time or aerodynamic efficiency turning round to see where Bill is. I dab the brakes later than ever then throw the bike on its side for the high speed entry to the Parabolica. Back on the throttle earlier than ever, screwing it open so hard I'm in danger of wrenching it off. I want every ounce of power the engine can give me to carry me to the line.

It turns out that when I cross it I'm way ahead of Bill. He tells me afterwards that he was a bit taken aback when I pulled alongside him, thinking he had more of a lead. But he also understands about the yellow flag, which is decent of him.

I ride around on the slowing down lap, feeling exhilarated and waving at the crowd, which is not huge but decent. Finally I pull into the pit lane. Syd is at the far end. You can't miss him, he's wearing a bright green Hawaiian shirt and purple braces. Normally he wears a jacket but it's in excess of forty degrees in the shade and I'm sweating like mad inside my leathers. I pull up to him. He is wearing a huge grin. I hand him the bike and, without even removing my helmet, casually whisper in his ear, 'Now who's a bloody good rider?'

To cap it all off I have a treasured picture of me on the top step of the podium, looking down at Bill. I don't fully realise it at the time, but I've just consciously exercised my power as a creator god.

Two weeks later at the Pre-TT Classic it rains harder than I've ever seen anywhere. Bill and I are miles in the lead in the 350cc race. He is much lighter so gets out of the three really slow corners much faster than I can, but I catch him through some of the faster stuff and on the brakes. On the last lap I'm taking way too many risks for the conditions but the 'red mist' is down and I'm determined. It is going to need one last almighty lunge on the brakes into the final corner, then baulk him enough on the way out that just maybe I can hang on to the line.

I don't get that far. I come through the fast penultimate corner about as quick as I would in the dry, and on the way out while still banked over the front tyre cries enough. Luckily I slide down the road on my ass instead of hitting the stone wall by the side of the track. There is actually a picture of me in the lead – but I'm no longer on the bike. My fastest lap of the race was only seven seconds outside the dry lap record. Not clever, and lucky. Effort outweighing talent. But that's what can happen when you think you've got a lot to prove.

And no, I didn't visualise that last bit.

1996

a girl turns my head

'I've got to follow her!'

I am standing on Southampton High Street one weekday lunchtime, after meeting an old school friend for a drink. As a self-employed consultant I never normally imbibe on a mid-week lunchtime because I need to remain self-motivated, and I don't want to slide down a slippery slope. But I've had to drop my car off to have some work done so I'm making an exception.

Nor do I normally follow girls around. Despite a largely underserved reputation from my racing years as a bit of a ladies man, I don't chat them up left, right and centre. But this is different. I can only see her indistinctly because the street is wide. I can make out very little of her face, and nor is there anything particularly startling about her attire. At a guess she's in her late twenties. She does have an unusual, almost jaunty gait, but that hardly explains the strange compunction that takes me over when she walks into a downstairs bar opposite. Something inside me is insistently urging me to follow her.

We cross the road and descend the stairs. I already know it's predominantly a student place, but it's not busy. Perhaps they do work during the day, or maybe they're all still in bed. She is standing at the bar, ordering a single drink. Scanning the room I'm pretty sure she hasn't come here to meet anyone, so I approach and stand right next to her. I don't remember who starts the conversation but within half an hour Sarah is telling me that we once shared a life together in the fabled 'Atlantis'. It sounds like complete nonsense, but something about her is drawing me in. It is irresistible.

After I left school I took a gap year in which, instead of travelling the world and broadening my horizons like any sensible young chap, I went to work for Hambros merchant bank in the city of London. Really. I rose to the heady ranks of supervisor in their Credit Analysis department. This wasn't appreciated by my newly subordinate colleagues who were already in their mid-twenties, although in large part their displeasure was more down to the fact that many of them had only got the job because daddy was a wealthy shipping magnate.

Apart from being invited to the odd party where

I felt completely out of my depth, about the only useful thing I can remember from this time is teaching them all to pretend they were doing handbrake turns in a car when walking around the office – and doing it myself one day as I came out of the lift and 'squealed' round the corner straight into the chairman. He wasn't amused.

During this time I lived in a rented flat in Camberwell with an old school friend, Jim. It wasn't the most salubrious area back in those days, and our idea of a good night out was to go to the new McDonalds in Piccadilly and have a Big Mac. Our landlady was a very warm-hearted African lady who loved cats, but we came home after a weekend away to find she'd kindly laid one of her old carpets in our living room – and the smell of cat urine was so bad we could hardly breathe. Nevertheless being a couple of polite ex-public schoolboys we didn't complain. We just left. Fairly sharpish.

After that I lived with my sister Pam for a while in her lovely flat in Queensgate Mews, until we fell out because I kept stealing her copy of *Motor Cycle News* before she'd had a chance to read it. She and I had an affinity in that we were the only members of our family who escaped Southampton and moved to the capital, and for many years she was the real 'belle of the ball', dating many famous and highly eligible bachelors – but, perhaps sadly, never marrying any of them.

After my gap year I stayed in the capital to study economics at University College. I just about scraped the exam grades I needed to get in. In fact I'd originally attempted to get into Oxford to read politics, philosophy and economics – for some reason I had visions of being an intellectual, enjoying heavy philosophical discussions with my fellow students 'til late into the night. But I didn't make it. Of course this was only because I was wrongly advised to apply to Balliol College, which had a fairly sporty reputation, when all I'd ever done in that regard was stroke the Colts 'B team' rowing eight. Nothing to do with just not being bright enough.

So instead I ended up sharing a student flat in Edgware with Bill, Pete and Les, who all loved a drink and took great pleasure in teaching me the trade. Les, a blunt northerner, had a reputation for drinking so much he regularly fell over – but his pint would always remain unspilt, and he'd be hugely insulted if offered a hand up. Bill would do anything he was told once he'd had a few drinks, which meant we were regularly on the floor too as he got slapped by just about every girl in College. Meanwhile Pete, who had the gift of the gab, was the centre of any pranks – of which there were so many they would fill their own book.

I had loved economics at school, mainly because we had a teacher who really enthused us. But as so often happens the same wasn't true of my university professors, and with only a few hours of lectures a week we had way too much spare time, only putting in any real effort when exams loomed. It was no great surprise when we all got lower second-class degrees.

But this too was just enough to get me into one of the big accountancy firms in London, Ernst and Young. This career path was chosen mainly by Syd and Pam, who for years had both been telling me what a great career it would be, while I still couldn't think of anything better to do. The work itself as a trainee auditor wasn't overly memorable, except I can recall being asked to oversee elections for the Milk Marketing Board in Thames Ditton – where the counting of votes only required about two hours work a day, meaning that I and my colleague Tony used to spend most of our time in the various pubs by the river.

The bespectacled Tony was something of the office clown, who could play the 'William Tell Overture' on his teeth, and nearly got the sack in his first week for leaving a pile of confidential audit files on the pavement while he went in search of a trolley – just as a senior partner turned up. But all that belied an intelligence that saw him end up as a big-shot in various financial institutions in the Far East. At one point he was even boss of the infamous Nick Leeson before the latter brought down Barings Bank.

By contrast the exams were really hard. Each year we used to have to spend six or seven weeks cramming at a college immediately beforehand, with endless three-hour mock papers. This wasn't helped when I turned up on the first Monday morning of one final cramming session with a broken right wrist sustained the previous day while racing. It was nice to provide my workmates with such hilarity, although not so clever when my efforts to learn to write with my left hand – fast and under pressure – proved fruitless and I failed. That meant another whole year before a retake.

In any case after I eventually passed I told my boss I wanted to leave. Selling computer software and hardware was all the rage, and several of my friends were making a fortune and having great fun into the bargain. I was amazed when he almost begged me to remain. He even guaranteed me a partnership before I was thirty, which was very rare. Of course this wasn't because I was a particularly brilliant accountant, it was just that they were starting to recognise the importance of having characters in the team who could relate to clients on a human level. My word I'd have been a wealthy man if I'd stayed – but would I have had the interesting life I've had? Probably not. So no regrets.

That is how at the beginning of 1986 I found myself working for the software division of Thorn EMI, going through the most rigorous sales training imaginable. They had the foresight to realise that you can teach someone with a professional background to sell, and they'll probably end up more successful than a pure salesperson. But my god did they put me through it. There would be days when at least an hour would be blocked out for me to sit in a room on my own and practice ‘cold calling’ one of the sales managers in another room. One in particular always turned me into a nervous wreck – like as not he would cut me off before I’d even finished saying ‘good afternoon’ because I hadn’t quite said it right.

But I guess it was all worth it, because it wasn’t too long before I wasn’t so much trying to attract new business as managing some of the best accounts we had. I think initially I was just in the right place at the right time, but I still had to perform, and once I was bedded in I found I could easily exceed my targets while only really working two or three days a week. That was where I learned the truth of the old adage about working smarter rather than harder.

Of course this was the materially-obsessed Thatcher era of ‘Yuppies’ with sharp suits and mullet haircuts earning way too much money and behaving like crushing bores. Sad to say my friends and I could have been poster boys for that stereotype, congregating at Yuppie headquarters, the infamous White Horse on Parson’s Green. But I must admit that we did have a ball. I was also lucky enough to end up as the company's top worldwide salesman three years running – much to the chagrin of some of my overseas colleagues especially, who would think they'd really cracked it each year, only for me to turn up at our annual sales awards in exotic locations like Cairo, Monaco and so on and take the spoils.

Yet invariably that which comes easily can mean very little. Winning a motorcycle race, even if only at club level, gave me far more satisfaction than any glittering sales award. I guess it's also about priorities. I loved the money I was earning, but I didn't *need* it – it wasn't as if I had a family to support. So it was pretty much easy come, easy go. In fact in my final year at Thorn, when I earned more than six figures, I was still in debt at the end of it.

This wasn't just high living though. It was at the beginning of 1989, as I approached the ripe old age of thirty and had had enough of hurting myself on two wheels, that I switched to the comparative safety but huge expense of four.

Forget motorcycle Grand Prix, British Touring Cars was now my real aim. In order to get there I entered a new championship for novice drivers called the Porsche Challenge. My chosen weapon was a white 1974 911 Carrera that cost me around £10,000 from memory, although I then spent several thousand more having it converted to the far better known 1973 'RS' version. This car remains my favourite of all time despite all the more modern machinery that has emerged in the interim, and it would now be worth several hundred thousand if I'd kept it, but there you go. Syd had had a tangerine orange version of this car when it first came out, which was what started my love affair with the marque. He had followed this up with a bright red 911 Turbo, the very first one ever imported into the country in 1974 as a factory demonstrator.

I did ok from the start, finishing on the podium in my first race despite having no brakes. Then a few months into the season Syd and I were talking one day when he dropped the bombshell that his Turbo was actually a lightened prototype that had been built in the factory race shop! I was already winning the odd races, but I figured that in his car I'd be unbeatable.

We arranged a test day with both cars at

Goodwood in Sussex, and on the way down we agreed we'd get alongside each other on the dual carriageway at 100 mph then, at a signal from me, accelerate hard. Syd's road car left my modified car choking in its dust. I couldn't wait to get to the circuit and strap him into the passenger seat so he could see what I could do with his pride and joy.

This didn't go quite as planned. His car's handling was all over the place and I was struggling to hang onto it, sideways everywhere. The brakes seemed awful too. I also put it down to me just taking time to warm up, but then what looked like a road-going Ford Sierra Cosworth came past us and this was just too much to bear. I got right up behind it on the next straight and left my braking late to go up the inside. Not only did the brakes somewhat object to this treatment but, with the car only having a rather primitive four-speed gearbox, I managed to select fourth not second as we sped into the corner. With no proper drive to the rear wheels the back end came serenely round and I fought it with opposite lock for as long as I could before admitting defeat, turning into the spin and off onto the grass.

Considering all his own racing experience I was surprised to see Syd as white as a sheet and shaking like a leaf. After all, his car was intact! I insisted that the problem was his brakes, tyres and suspension just weren't set up for the track, and if he came out with me in my car we'd lap ten seconds a lap faster with no drama at all. But he was having none of it. Incidentally, I later found out that the Cosworth was on much faster slick tyres, but never mind.

On another memorable occasion, when Syd was driving up to Snetterton in his car to see me race, he got into a 'dice' with another fast car on the way. On all the radio news the next day was how amazed police were to stop a red Porsche doing 120mph, only to find that the driver was in his seventies and wearing a cloth cap. Of course this only served as a proud addition to his endless store of anecdotes.

Unlike the following incident, which didn't show him in such a good light. My parents were members of the Porsche Owners Club and used to attend the main weekend get together each year. They would drive to different places in their cars, then stop and have lunch or whatever. Of course Syd didn't particularly like driving in convoy, so he would sometimes hang back so he could 'boot' the throttle and show everyone how fast he was.

On this occasion he did so just as my mother was bending down to reach a knitting needle on the passenger floor – yes, she used to knit while they were driving along. Not ready for the sideways jerk as her beloved threw the car into a left-handed corner, she fell across into his lap and somehow got her head stuck under the steering wheel so he couldn't straighten it on the way out of the bend. The last that was seen of them they were heading off into the forest with mother in a somewhat compromising position.

Another particularly embarrassing episode from this period occurred at another of these Porsche Owners Club weekends, which this time I attended along with my then girlfriend Helena. She was an intelligent girl, whose attractiveness certainly wasn't diminished by being a part-time underwear model to boot. After a fairly heavy night we came down to breakfast rather late to find my mother chatting amicably to a pair of complete strangers.

We joined them and talked a little about how I was competing in the race series, then I made what turned out to be the fatal mistake of mentioning that I might pop over to the merchandise stand to buy myself an umbrella. At this my mother insisted she should pay for it. I thanked her but politely insisted there was no need because I had a good job and could comfortably manage the whole transaction myself. At which point she came out with the most unexpected sentence I – and I'm pretty sure anyone else alive or dead – has ever heard: 'I spoil him because I feel guilty for having him circumcised as a baby.'

Where the f*^k did that come from?!! Could we not have discussed this before in private?!! I got up, took Helena's hand, nodded sheepishly at the wide-eyed couple and walked away. Again there just weren't any words.

Back with the racing itself, I won the Challenge championship in my second year, and so for the 1991 season I decided to put all my efforts into the more professional Porsche Supercup. The trouble was I spent everything I had getting the top team to prepare the car for me over the winter – the interior had to be stripped right out, the engine tuned, the suspension changed because we would be running on slicks, and so on – meaning I then had very little money left to actually run it. What is more my nephew Mike was my only mechanic, but at sixteen he had about as much idea how to prepare a race car as I did.

We weren't short of laughs though, especially staying in my van in the paddock. With me in relative luxury on a fold-out double airbed and him crammed down between the spare wheels and toolboxes underneath, we used to amuse ourselves by making up childish rhymes about the other drivers before we went to sleep. Except when I had Helena with me too, which required a bit of diplomacy in such a tight space.

But we were as professional as we could be given the circumstances. On slick tyres it became especially important to know whether the suspension settings were correct, which meant checking the temperature readings across the width of each tyre as soon as I came in from practice. Not that we knew how to change the settings, but at least we knew if they were wrong.

The competition to set a good time in order to be high up on the grid was far greater now than it had been too. The tyres were only really at their best on about the second or third laps before they overheated and we had to pull in to rest them. Couple that with the fact all the top guys would go testing at each circuit during the week before, whereas I couldn't afford that, plus I'd never been to any of them on slicks before, and we were right up against it. I even introduced a new rule of no alcohol for forty-eight hours before a meeting, just so I'd be as sharp as possible, especially during practice.

One of my team mates was championship-leading Kiwi Craig Simmiss, who'd done really well in Formula 3 previously so knew what he was about. He realised I was facing a steep learning curve so, halfway through the season at Donington Park, he told me to try and slot in behind him during practice when we were on our second runs. I warned Mike and Helena that, whatever they were doing at the time, if I saw Craig coming down the pit lane behind me and started revving the engine, they were to let go of everything because I was just about to blast off after him.

I duly followed Craig but his car was handling so much better than mine it was hard to stick right with him for more than a few corners. Worse still, when I came back in and enquired after Helena, Mike told me she was in the medical centre with a broken hand. Apparently she hadn't fully heeded my warning and had been checking a rear tyre pressure with her other hand in front of the wheel as I drove off. Of course I apologised but I'm not sure that we lasted too long after that.

Nevertheless towards the end of the season our little team started showing what it could do, especially after I got a suspension upgrade at Brands Hatch and stormed to third place overall. By the end of the season, fifth place in Class A of the championship was no mean feat, and on that basis a satellite team offered to run my car the following year for no payment. I was over the moon. Until a call came through the night before our first practice day that a wealthy driver wanted to join the team, but wouldn't do so if I was in it – knowing that I would beat him.

That was that really. At the start of the new season I claimed fifth place at Silverstone, but was still having to overdrive a poorly prepared car. Then a high-speed excursion onto the grass at the next meeting at Thruxton, where I was lucky not to write it off, made my mind up. There was no point carrying on without proper backing.

I left Thorn in 1989 because I and two colleagues decided to set up our own IT consultancy company with the grand title of Executive Information Solutions Ltd, or EISL for short. Our aim was to design and install information systems for senior executives in major blue-chip companies. Nick and I had always been close since the day we first met on an internal training course, while Jon was the controlling partner because, rather handily, his father-in-law just happened to be the chairman of one of the largest manufacturing conglomerates in the UK – so he would be using his contacts to introduce most of our business. We did well and expanded rapidly over several years, but neither Nick or I was happy with the way the company was being run – Jon had a somewhat dictatorial, bullying style with the rest of the staff.

Eventually I said enough was enough and early

in 1992 I left to go out on my own, even though I was now in pretty desperate financial straights after racing cars for three years. It may sound irresponsible or just plain stupid to have spent all my money in that way, but remember I was pursuing a dream, I did have at least some talent, and I'd done everything I could to attract backing from elsewhere. I even invited a whole load of our clients to a hospitality suite at Silverstone, but in pouring rain my windscreen wipers decided to pack up just before the race started. It was an old car and one of the hidden nuts that held the drive mechanism together had worked loose over the years.

So although I'd now made the decision to stop racing, the debts had already mounted up. To add to this I'd bought a wonderful open-plan maisonette in Fulham some years before, but had then re-mortgaged it to invest in a small, sixteenth-century, mill worker's cottage by the River Avon in Saltford, between Bath and Bristol – just before the huge property crash. So now I had two properties with negative equity, a huge overdraft, no guaranteed income – and my mother had just passed on after suffering a stroke not long after her seventieth birthday.

I think she just gave up on life. Syd had remained busy preparing race bikes in his workshop at home, but he'd lie in bed all morning and then work late into the night – which meant in her latter years my mother was often left alone in the evening, sitting in her conservatory doing jigsaw puzzles and the like. Of course they used to go to family gatherings and various car-and-bike-related events together, but she'd still confided in me how lonely she was not long before her death.

I have already said what an incredible, resourceful, loving woman my mother was. Unfortunately being the youngest I was her favourite, and it was shamefully easy to take her for granted. But I always remember her telling me how her family had been so poor when she was young that she always had to wear her older sister Joy's hand-me-downs to school, where the other children would make fun of her. It still breaks my heart to write that now.

I am not disrespecting her memory in saying she was no great intellectual, but her life revolved around bringing up and giving unlimited love to her six children, and then fostering around thirty more when I was just a kid. Almost certainly she was valiantly and selflessly trying to make sure that we and all the other little ones had a better childhood than she did.

It didn't help her loneliness that some five years before my sister Sheila had been tragically killed in a car crash that wasn't her fault, leaving two young children. She was a wonderful 'child of nature' who would help anyone, and she loved animals so much she set up her own cattery. It was a terrible blow because I loved her very much, but somehow I accepted that in a family of our size some early loss might be inevitable – except we might have expected it to be me or Barry, who deliberately risked our lives racing. In any case her husband had remarried and relations had become strained to the point where they suddenly cut off all my parents' contact with their grandchildren. I think this was the straw that broke the camel's back for my mother.

She suffered an initial stroke and seemed to be not too bad when I first rushed down from London to see her, but she then entered a coma from which she never emerged. To make matters worse the doctors and nurses in the cottage hospital near the family home in

Romsey had the typical physically-oriented worldview common to many in their profession, so could be rather callous. For example they talked loudly in her room about how she wasn't aware of anything that was going on, and how they were going to take her off her life-supporting drip – before even discussing it with us, her family.

I don't think my atheism was quite as strong by this time. I had gradually developed something of an interest in 'alternative history' – I can definitely remember being enraptured by Eric von Daniken's infamous *Chariots of the Gods* – and I would often lie awake and ponder questions such as whether there was intelligent life elsewhere in the universe. I remember I felt that if there *was* then the chance of it all emerging just by chance and natural evolution was significantly reduced, because it wouldn't have just occurred on our one little rock in our one little solar system.

So even though I didn't have a strong spiritual worldview yet, I nevertheless had a very strong sense that mother had at least some awareness of her surroundings even when in coma. So as a family we insisted that we leave her room if the doctors wanted to discuss her case.

We all took it in turns to watch over her, and about five days after she went into coma I sat reading to her one night while holding her hand. I will always remember how a teardrop slowly formed in the corner of one of her eyes, and she almost imperceptibly squeezed my hand. The professionals said these were just nervous reactions. I guarantee you they weren't. The following day she took her final leave, and I like to think she found a peace and freedom she hadn't had for some time.

Her funeral was far better attended than any of us expected – we simply hadn't realised that she was probably as popular among the motorcycle racing fraternity as Syd himself. I lost count of the number of people, former world champions and all, who came up to me and said what an effect she'd had on them and how much they'd admired and loved her. As you can imagine, that meant a hell of a lot.

Not long after this I sold all my properties in an attempt to sort out my financial situation, and moved to rural Leicestershire where my good friend Doug from university days had bought an idyllic cottage. But I simply couldn't attract any consultancy work, despite serious efforts, and I was forced to go bankrupt.

I remember going to see my bank manager before I left London and asking him how he could justify the usury of charging me 33.3% interest on the excess of my overdraft over its agreed limit – and how exactly that was supposed to help my efforts to get out of the hole I'd got myself into. He just shrugged, and I thought, 'I'll sort out all my personal debts, but if that's your attitude your bank can go whistle for its money.' As for bankruptcy itself, it's quite something to have to argue to be allowed to hang onto the last forty pounds you have in the whole world, along with a crappy old car and a computer needed for potential work. I also remember how in those dark days cigarettes came before food every time.

At the beginning of 1993 I moved back to Southampton to live with Syd who, knowing he'd never been cut out to look after himself, was now on a dating website, claiming to be way younger than he was and attracting all the wrong women by emphasising that he had a bright red Porsche Turbo.

Although things were still difficult financially, one wonderful memory from that summer is competing at the inaugural Festival of Speed, a hill climb through the grounds of Goodwood House. Syd was invited to prepare his big 444cc Aermacchi for me to ride, and although I was no longer competing on two or four wheels it was too good an opportunity to miss.

We arrived early on the Saturday so I could walk up and learn the course, never having seen it before. Remember a hill climb is very different from circuit racing, because each time you only get a single run – in this case two in practice on the Saturday then two race runs on the Sunday. I found it hard to believe I was the only competitor in a car or on a bike who took the trouble to walk the hill, but it was just as well I did. Not only was I a little rusty but, despite Syd's normal reputation for preparing fast and reliable bikes, our gear change lever broke as I went away from the line at the start of the first practice run. So I only had one trip up the hIll before race day.

Talking of which this was a tragic affair, because

one of the last riders up got into a huge wobble as he crossed the finish line, then fell off and was killed – supposedly hitting his head on a tree trunk. We were being held in a field at the top of the course, along with the historic Formula 1 drivers who had ascended before us. The only way to return to the pits was back down the same way, and we all had to wait for several hours while the police attended the scene to measure skid marks and so on.

This was an absolute tragedy for the event Lord March had worked so hard to create, causing adverse publicity just at the wrong time. Of course it was a tragedy for the rider who lost his life too, and for his family, but it later emerged that he'd had a heart attack as he crossed the line. I saw the tree that was supposed to have killed him, it was no more than a sapling with a tiny nick in it.

In the meantime there we were at the top of the hill oblivious to all this. It will sound strange to the modern ear but in those days mobile phones were like bricks, and anyway coverage was poor. But at least there was a veritable feast of celebrities. The boss of the Mclaren F1 team, Ron Dennis, was having his first drive in one on their early cars, while eventually world champion Damon Hill managed to find a way to get up to us via the back roads and told us what was going on.

Meanwhile I was sitting astride my bike talking to a very nice chap about cricket. He responded to my question about his line of work with 'the music business'. It turned out it was Matt Aitken, one of the trio of immensely successful music producers who brought us acts such as Rick Astley. I of course thanked him profusely for furnishing us with such delights, while he responded with a grin that he didn't really care about the quality of the music if it allowed him to indulge his passion for historic F1 cars, among other things.

I also met a very attractive woman driver at the top of the hill, even persuading her to sit astride my ageing, oily machine so I could take a break – there weren't any trees to lean it up against. I also joined her and her sadly equally charming husband that night at the champagne reception Lord March threw for all of us competitors in Goodwood House, drinking with them 'til the early hours.

For some reason I'd agreed to stay in the back of the van at the top of the paddock while Syd and Mike were in a plush hotel. The following morning the bikes were the first race up the hill, so I poked my head out at about 7.30am, but nothing was happening. Feeling somewhat the worse for wear I went back to sleep. Unfortunately I awoke about an hour later to hear a load of bikes being warmed up. I threw my leathers and boots on, grabbed mine out of the van and ran it down to the holding area – where they had already let all the others across the circuit to go down to the startline, but refused to let me join them.

Older bikes need to have their engines warmed up thoroughly before you race them otherwise they break piston rings, so there I was revving up my lone, loud Aermacchi while the announcer tried to make himself heard to what was a crowd of over twenty thousand even in that inaugural year. There were more celebrities everywhere, including ex-Beetle George Harrison who had come down in a small but very fast, bike-engined car. The wife of a fellow competitor – guessing I might have had a heavy night – kindly brought me over a strong black coffee, while others argued with the marshals to let me across, with eventual success.

Unsurprisingly I wasn't overly quick in that first timed run, but I learned the course a little better, and by the afternoon had sobered up enough to set the fastest time of the day for the bikes – albeit that we could have gone much quicker with more practice. Later as I walked up to receive the trophy from Lord March I had to walk past Syd, who was chatting away to some people, and as I did I heard him say, 'Good Old Ian'. Not sure about the old, but that was one of the few times I ever actually heard him being complementary about my riding, rather than having to hear it from someone else – and it meant a lot.

Even more surprising was when we all received a complimentary video of the day in the post. John Surtees is the only man ever to have won blue riband world championships on both two and four wheels, a feat that will surely never be repeated. He had been due to ride at the event and was still pretty rapid desplte advancing years, but he fell off in practice and broke his wrist, leaving him unable to race. In the bike section of the video they simply mention his name as they show a clip of him riding up the hill, shortly before showing a clip of yours truly dubbed over with 'and here comes the *maestro* Ian Lawton'. Undeserved but much appreciated praise, and I didn't even pay them! What is more I remain the lap record holder in perpetuity, because the bikes were never again allowed a properly timed race after that first year's tragic fatality.

Returning to Syd's romantic life, eventually he met a very nice lady called Joan who wasn't just after his money, and they had a great time together until he broke his hip in a fall during a holiday in the US. He was never the same after that and, despite proudly telling me many years before that if he was ever about to lose his marbles he would drive his car into a motorway parapet, he succumbed to Alzheimer's. The trouble is by the time it has happened it's too late to take control.

Luckily he didn't get the scared, don't-know-where-I-am version, it was more like reverting to childhood. His short-term memory was shot, and often when we went to see him he didn't really know who we were. He would regularly take one of his favourite Black Magic chocolates out of the box, forget it was in his hand resting on his lap, and end up with melted chocolate everywhere.

As is so often the case though his long-term memory was intact, and under prompting he could tell us things like what main jet he had in the carburettor on his works Norton at such-and-such a race in the 1950s. These glimpses of the old Syd were wonderful but became rarer, and to me at least it felt something of a blessing when he too decided enough was enough and left us early in 1997.

One thing I'll always remember is how his eyes, which had always had a magic 'twinkle' in them, were almost completely lifeless for his last few days. What I know *now* is that his soul was almost certainly departing on a regular basis to check out conditions wherever he was headed, before he made the final leap. In these relatively relaxed conditions I suspect the soul can make its own choices about when and how to leave the body.

Nevertheless, just as with the passing of my sister and mother some years beforehand, none of this prompted me into a full-blown spiritual conversion or crisis. Having said that I'm pretty sure that each loss led me more towards the view that death wasn't the end, even if only in a very broad sense. Nor did it seem to me that I was just believing it because it might make me feel better.

As for my own life, things continued to be very tight for at least a year after I moved back home. I decided to teach myself Microsoft's Visual Basic programming language, so I could perhaps develop some software applications myself and also have a better technical understanding when I was managing IT projects. Almost immediately I saw a gap in the market for a modelling system that could be used easily by senior executives and managers, allowing them to input various assumptions about exchange and interest rates, sales volumes, costs and so on into a budgeting and forecasting system that could be used right across a large organisation.

This was actually based on my experiences of undertaking consultancy work for another of the UK's largest manufacturing conglomerates while I was with EISL. Operating in fluctuating global markets as they did and needing to make decisions fast, I knew this was exactly what they needed – rather than having to wait for analysts to prepare spreadsheets to look at different scenarios.

It turns out that programming is extremely addictive, and I would often work sixteen or more hours a day – much to the annoyance of my then girlfriend Maggie when I went to stay with her in London – on what I called, fairly obviously, the Business Modeller. The fascinating thing is the logic. You develop some code, you debug it, and then it still doesn't do exactly what you want it to do. Now at that point you can either get seriously angry and threaten to throw your computer out of the window, which is most people's initial reaction, or you can grow to accept that this is an entirely logical system that will do exactly what you program it to do. So if something is wrong there must be an error in your design or your programming, and not – at least for a beginner like me – in the software.

After about six months of intensive work I had perfected the system, and was ready to show it to my old contacts at the aforementioned company. I had kept them informed of what I was doing and I knew they were interested. I got as far as a meeting with the Group Finance Director, who was favourably impressed. But in the final reckoning he decided that for political reasons it couldn't be rolled out across the whole group, so we couldn't go ahead.

I was devastated. I had produced marketing materials and demonstrated it at a few exhibitions and seminars, but in truth I'd really been putting all my eggs in that one basket. Perhaps it was a weakness that I gave up on the system not long afterwards. But in retrospect I've always felt that it may have just been a little ahead of its time.

I had a visit from my two brothers John and Barry during this difficult period. They were clearly spokesmen for the rest of the family, asking why I didn't get a 'proper job' and stop living rent-free off our father. They weren't being horrible, they just couldn't get their heads round the fact that, if I started earning a salary or wages, almost all of it would be automatically deducted by the court to pay my creditors – mainly the bank who, remember, I had no qualms about. Whereas if I was self employed it all worked very differently. So I persevered in the determination that more work would come my way somehow or other.

It will be easy to understand that when I meet Sarah I'm at something of a crossroads in my life. By this time I've proved my brothers wrong and the consultancy work has been flowing in nicely for several years. Indeed I've just been able to purchase a lovely cottage in the picturesque yachting village of Hamble, just outside Southampton. But I'm no longer racing and I've found nothing I really care about to replace it. I am ripe for something new, and she's providing it.

Actually when we first meet I'm seeing someone else and, truth be told, initially I'm not that physically attracted to her. Without wishing to sound arrogant she comes on pretty strong but for the most part I resist her, at least in the early days. Yet I'm increasingly fascinated by the things she talks about, things that I've never even considered. In our very first meeting she tells me, 'You need to *feel* more, listen to your *intuition* and your *heart*, stop always *thinking* with your *head*.' No one has ever said anything like that to me before.

I scarcely even know what intuition is at first, but she recommends James Redfield's seminal *Celestine Prophecy* and I can't get enough of it. It has introduced so many millions of people around the world to a spiritual worldview and, while many with more experience scoff at some of the ideas and writing, I still maintain it's gold dust for a complete newcomer. Not that everyone would be as gullible as me and actually assume it's a true story all the way through, so that by the end I genuinely want to travel to South America to search for the so-called 'tenth insight' myself. I am so deflated when Sarah tells me it's just a novel.

Incidentally it's important to make a distinction between a *spiritual* worldview and a *religious* one. Broadly speaking the former simply accepts that there's more to existence than just the material world we perceive around us, but doesn't follow any particular set of teachings and allows people to make up their own minds about what to believe.

By contrast the latter tends to involve following

some sort of fixed set of teachings or even dogma. Although orthodox religions like Christianity, Judaism, Islam, Hinduism and so on are still followed by millions around the world, especially in the West people have been deserting them in their droves in search of a more flexible and personally meaningful approach. As far as I'm concerned this isn't before time. Note also that spirituality in general shouldn't be confused with 'spiritualism', which is a specific approach that most obviously uses mediums to make contact with the dead.

In any case it takes around a year before Sarah finally persuades me that we should be together and I should end my other relationship. Part of the deal for me is that when I finally give in it means I'm accepting that everything she's been telling me about lives together in Atlantis and so on is true – or at least that she genuinely believes it and isn't just using it as a lure – and moreover that I'm now prepared to be open to it all.

In the meantime I've been becoming more and more frustrated with my consultancy work. A good friend from my Thorn days who also set up his own company, Phil, has been using me as an experienced but part-time project manager for some time. My old pal Nick from EISL has also joined him. But Phil understandably wants to promote people into project manager roles from within. One chap in particular who is assisting me on a large project decides he will try and play politics, going behind my back and trying to drop me in it whenever he can because he has designs on my job.

Things come to a head one day and I go to see Phil. I can completely see why he needs to side with people who work for him full time, even though I'm sure he realises I will be a loss to him. So I call time. Coupled with meeting Sarah who is opening up whole new avenues of thought for me, the allure of the commercial world has faded. I just can't take its preoccupation with money, contracts, deals, deadlines, targets, progress, success and so on any more – and this kind of office politics is just the final straw. I want to devote more time to the big questions in life.

Of course many people think I must have lost several marbles from my already small collection, but my intuitive inner voices are pretty insistent that this is the right thing to do –

and now I've learned to listen to them. I am sure many other people hear similar inner voices and would love to have the time to research the mysteries of life, but are prevented from so doing by family and other commitments that I don't have. If it helps all I can say is that, as we'll see, the grass isn't always greener.

Indeed if I'd properly appreciated the financial hardships and other frustrations in advance, I might have tried harder to shut the voices out.

1998

the search for truth begins

We are at the top of the Grand Gallery, deep inside the Great Pyramid of Giza in Egypt. Quietly and slowly we climb up the ladder, one rung at a time. At the top we stop briefly to don our head torches. We are high above the floor, nearly thirty feet up. Thankfully the ladder is tied to the wall, because it's steeply inclined. In perhaps the scariest part of the operation we lever ourselves off and into the passage, and begin the crawl towards our goal. The loose stones on the floor scrape at our exposed knees, but we hardly notice.

At the end of the passage we come out into a small chamber in which we can stand. We see that a succession of short ladders lead up to the higher chambers, but we must ignore these for the moment. Our target lies ahead. We have to lie on our sides to squeeze through the narrow slit which gives access to the first chamber, Davison's.

As we pick ourselves up, our torches reveal a long low room matching the size of the King's Chamber beneath it. There is some rubble in the far corner, and the unevenness of the floor blocks is in stark contrast to the smoothness of the monolithic ceiling blocks. But as our heads turn to the corner nearest us on our left, our torches reveal what we have come to explore. A passage leading off to the side.

We know this exploratory passage was excavated by Captain Caviglia in the nineteenth century. But rumours have been abounding for several years that it's been extended to look for a secret chamber. We have been told on the grapevine that supposedly eminent researchers have been sharing video footage of this secret excavation, all under strict non-disclosure agreements. Many people have suggested this is the real reason why the Pyramid has been closed to the public for some time now, although the official line is that essential renovation work is being carried out. We must discover the truth.

We scramble towards it, excitement mounting. Crawling inside, we can see that after about ten feet it turns sharp right to follow the south wall of the chamber, heading west. Faster now... we must get to the corner to see where it leads. Peering around we can see that the passage extends for a further fifteen feet or so, but by the time we're halfway along we can already see what lies ahead. We have waited so long for this moment. Now we know the truth...

The passage ends in a blank wall!

After I give up my consulting work I have some money put by – not a great deal, but enough to see me through for a while – and plenty of time on my hands. Sarah has pretty much moved into my cottage by now and we've been reading an alternative magazine called *Quest for Knowledge*. It isn't not long before I see they're looking for a new editor and, for some reason, having no qualifications for the job whatsoever doesn't seem to put me off. I phone the publisher but he says he's just appointed a chap called Chris Ogilvie-Herald. But he advises me to call him to see if I can help in any way.

When Chris enquires what sort of stuff I'm into I can only think of crop circles, because Sarah and I have been visiting a few over the summer. He says that would be fine, why don't I prepare an article about them as the magazine hasn't covered the topic for a while? So it is, quite unexpectedly, that my career as a writer and researcher begins. I would never have dreamed of undertaking truly original research before, even in my university days, but for some unknown reason I'm now emboldened and feel I can give this a good go.

I really throw myself into the task, emailing people left, right and centre, finding out everything I can from the fledgling internet, reading books. Eventually I complete my article and I'm very proud of it. Given the wealth of evidence on the 'Circlemakers' website – with pictures of them actually creating some famous formations, showing all the tools they use and exactly how they do it – I come to the conclusion that most crop circles are man-made, and that the simplest versions may be the only genuine ones, if any. I email it to Chris and wait for the praise that will surely come.

It takes about a week for him to ring me, but when he does he has bad news. 'Ian, I simply can't publish it,' he says and, totally deflated, I enquire why not. 'Because it's about 12,000 frigging words long and would take up the entirety of about three issues!' he exclaims, and burst out laughing. I am so green I didn't even think to ask him if there was a word limit, nor have I paid any attention to how many I've been writing.

But there's a silver lining. Sarah and I go to several conferences, meet Chris in person and get on well. For an ex-squaddy who hasn't had the benefit of my expensive education – as he would never tire of telling me – he has a sharp mind and seems to know a lot of people in the alternative research world. Soon after he calls me.

'How would you like to write a book about the pyramids at Giza with me?'

'Why me?' I ask.

'Because after that article I know you can write, and I can't,' is his typically candid response. It seems a great way into the business, so I accept straight away.

Chris really wants to concentrate on the politics of the Giza plateau, which is just outside Cairo and home not only to the Great Pyramid but also its two famous counterparts. A great deal of exploration has been going on there and a fevered atmosphere surrounds it. This is in no small part due to the prophecies of the mid-twentieth century American psychic Edgar Cayce, the 'sleeping prophet' who predicted that in 1998 a 'Hall of Records' would be uncovered there containing information about the lost civilisation of Atlantis.

Celebrated alternative authors such as Graham Hancock and Robert Bauval have been writing huge bestsellers about all this, concentrating in particular on a supposed correlation between the layout of the Giza pyramids and the three stars in Orion's Belt, and also questioning the age and purpose of the monuments. Sarah and I have been reading them and initially we're highly impressed.

Another author they reference is the world-renowned Zecharia Sitchin who, in his *Twelfth Planet* series, has been claiming to be the first person to properly decode various ancient Mesopotamian texts. He maintains that these show the human race to be the genetic creation of an ancient race of extraterrestrials called the 'Anunnaki', hailing from a twelfth planet in our solar system called 'Nibiru'. Again we initially find these ideas absolutely captivating, and hungrily devour as much of this material as we can.

After a little more thought I tell Chris that I understand almost nothing about the basics of the Giza pyramids. This despite the fact that I took a tour inside the Great Pyramid some years ago during a sales awards conference with Thorn – where I'm ashamed to say some of us were so hungover we had no recollection of the interior, we just knew we'd been there. So I insist that we must also include a proper treatise on the structure of the pyramids, and on who built them, when, why and how. This on top of the need to investigate the rumours that the Egyptian authorities are hunting for a secret chamber containing the 'Hall'.

In order to accomplish all this we agree that we'd better take a trip out there. A two-week stay is arranged for the autumn of 1998, and Chris makes some contacts who should be able to help us get inside the closed Great Pyramid in particular. I stock up on an army-style waistcoat with myriad pockets for penknives, notebooks, cameras, head torches and all the things I'll need for the exploration. Sarah starts to call me 'Indy' after the Harrison Ford character.

When we get out there two things strike the first-time visitor to the Giza plateau. First, just how *massive* these structures are. Pictures simply don't do them justice, nor does merely quoting the statistic that the Great Pyramid stands around 450 feet tall. Second, the scarcely believable fact that the infamous Sphinx sits looking out implacably from the eastern edge of the plateau – straight at a Kentucky Fried Chicken shop. Urban sprawl and a lack of proper planning has brought the suburbs of Cairo right to its doorstep.

We are staying in the village of Nazlet el-Samman next to the plateau, and we reach out to the contact who will help us get into the closed Pyramid, who runs one of the small perfumeries that abound here. Every morning we're instructed to be at his shop by 10am. Every morning we turn up, clothes bulging with equipment. The locals get used to us and decide to nickname me something I only later find out translates as 'silver fox', I guess because of my already greying hair. The trouble is every day, after waiting around for several hours, we're told it's a no-go. I have already handed over $500 because there are many intermediaries who have to be bribed and ready, and each day some problem prevents our expedition.

In the meantime we're far from idle. We manage to be escorted into the Sphinx enclosure, which is actually the most sacred space of them all to the locals. We dress up in galabayas, operating under cover of night and of a huge concert by the ageless singer Shirley Bassey in honour of President Mubarak's wife. This is happening close to the enclosure and on the plus side there's obviously plenty of noise, but the downside is there are lots of people around too.

We start in relative safety by investigating a tunnel cut into the Sphinx's rump, about which rumours have also been abounding. Here we find nothing but a relatively small passage crudely cut into the rock that goes both upwards and downwards for only around 15 feet, each time ending in a blank rock face. It may be a late-period tomb, or an even later exploration tunnel, but one thing for sure is there's nothing untoward or exciting about it. It certainly doesn't connect up with other structures on the Plateau as some researchers have been claiming.

The same is true when we up the ante and steal round to the front to investigate a supposed secret chamber behind the 'Dream Stela' of Thutmose IV, which nestles between the monument's front legs. We find that such a chamber does indeed exist but it's clearly an entirely modern addition, accessed by dropping down through a square opening in the roof – and it's tiny, only measuring about 5 feet in each direction. Again nothing secret, mysterious or untoward. In actual fact our guide is so nervous that I let Chris investigate and then choose not to add to the poor man's woes by going in myself. I can literally see his heart trying to jump out of his chest underneath his loose galabaya. As the last link in the chain he's probably only been paid a pittance, but he'll be the one who faces a lengthy jail stretch if we're caught. As foreigners we'd only be deported.

There is something else that preoccupies us. By now we know a great deal about the interior of the Great Pyramid, which contains two main rooms in the superstructure, the so-called King's and Queen's Chambers. They are connected by an ascending passage, the Grand Gallery, which has sloping sides so the roof more or less comes to a point around thirty feet from the floor. Our focus is to be able to enter the so-called

Relieving Chambers above the King's, which is where the supposed secret tunnelling has been going on.

These are accessed via an intrusive tunnel excavated by nineteenth-century explorers that starts at the top end of the Gallery – and, of course, we'll need a ladder to be there when we go in, otherwise our $500 will have been pretty much wasted. We know that sometimes it's there, sometimes it's not. We closely question people who've paid vast amounts of money to enter the Pyramid for officially sanctioned meditation sessions while it's been closed, but we can't gain a consistent picture. Some think yes, some think no.

In no time we're nearing the end of our fortnight stay. If the gods aren't with us today or tomorrow we'll be going home empty handed, so we're understandably nervous as we head for the shop. We wait several hours. It looks as if it's going to be no-go again. Then suddenly it's action stations and we *are* going in after all. Excitement mounts as we ascend the plateau towards the Pyramid – in broad daylight, so we're hardly adopting maximum stealth. The intimation that this really isn't that big a deal is confirmed when our guide stays at the entrance and doesn't even bother to come in with us. He gives us an hour.

We enter and climb up to the base of the Grand Gallery. Hallelujah! Looking up we can see that our prayers have been answered and the ladder is there. We ascend the steps and continue along the short horizontal passage into the King's Chamber. Here we find plenty of students from Cairo University who seem to be doing exactly the sort of restoration work we've been led to expect. They pay us little attention, which tells its own story. We pretend to look around for about five minutes then, aware that time is limited, we head back to the top of the Gallery.

There are now a couple of workers down at its base. We know it's now or never. Chris goes first. As he starts to ascend the ladder they look up, but again pay little attention. Their look seems to suggest 'stupid foreigners', of which they get more than their fair share. But imagine what would happen if we were in the UK – health and safety would have a field day!

What happened next has already been described at the beginning of this chapter. In fact that version of events is taken from the book we would eventually write, and uses a certain artistic licence. The intrusive passages are only just over three feet square so there's no way Chris and I can crawl down them together, and the ladder isn't robust enough to take two heavy men of over six feet. So he goes first and, after an anxious wait of around twenty minutes, returns to report nothing untoward. I go in second with my camera, notebook and so on.

It is extremely hot in the interior, and I've suffered from claustrophobia ever since, as a young child, my sister Sheila locked me in a small, dark cupboard and told me mummy and daddy would never find me. It sounds nasty but siblings fight, don't they? I forgave her a long time ago, but it has been a problem at times, especially in lifts. Yet in these cramped, hot, dusty passages, so small you can't even turn around, I'm as calm as anything. I guess it's because my mind is entirely focussed on the job at hand – on getting the pictures we need, and on making the appropriate detailed notes.

As those pictures will show, Caviglia dug a few feet in different directions when he got to the end of his tunnel, effectively allowing him to just about stand up, but it's absolutely clear that all we're seeing in every direction are his old chisel marks on the sandstone blocks that make up the bulk of the Pyramid's interior. Moreover we've already visited the British Library to consult detailed drawings by one of his successors, John Perring, which show the tunnel is still exactly as it was when originally excavated. It hasn't been even slightly extended in any direction. Caviglia didn't find any secret chambers, and no one has touched his tunnel since.

Which makes it all the more laughable that several well-known researchers, who claim to have been down this tunnel in person, are telling everyone on the internet that its previous endpoint has been recently extended by a further 25 to 30 feet. As we will go on to report in the book, clearly they felt in need of a little extra length. Talk about 'fake news'.

As soon as we get back to where we're staying I grab a siesta – it's been a habit with me for as long as I can remember. When I wake up I can feel I've got a description of our experience almost word for word as it needs to be written down. Chris is somewhat put out when I grab my notebook computer from him, but it's just as well I do because I know now that this kind of post-sleep inspiration must be acted on immediately. The words pour out effortlessly as I write what will become the introduction to the book from which the opening passage is taken – even though again I have to use poetic licence when I pretend we got into the Pyramid by tagging onto a night-time meditation group, to protect those who actually got us in.

As soon as we return home I prepare a synopsis-cum-proposal for the new book based mainly around this fairly arresting opening narrative. Chris arranges a meeting with a London literary agent of his acquaintance, who loves it and forwards it to several publishers. In no time Virgin Books have come back to us with an offer. The advance isn't huge, only £5000 each, but we're delighted to be getting published at all. We accept, with a deadline of six months time, and then the work really begins.

In truth the synopsis has painted a slightly false picture, considering it reads somewhat like an action thriller. The real first part of a book that will eventually extend to a total of nearly 400 pages comprises the rather more scholarly enquiry into the when, who, why and how of the pyramids as mentioned previously. We have always agreed that Chris will only be researching and drafting some of the more political chapters that appear later in the book, so I will have to write and research the entirety of the heavy first part – but, after all, it was me who said it needed this material. The internet is still in its relative infancy, but the good news is that Chris lives in north London, so each week I give him a list of all the books I need and he goes to the British Library and elsewhere to get them, after which we meet in the Fleet Services on the M3 for the handover.

I have an outline of the chapters I need to write, which is the majority, and I'm on a schedule of around two weeks for each one. The problem is I just haven't appreciated the huge volume of research I have to undertake, especially for the early chapters. Then there's the writing itself. Several of them turn out to be around 25,000 words long – which is about a third of the length suggested for an entire book by some publishers. But I'm determined to get this right, often by working between 16 and 18 hour days.

By the end I'm exhausted, and genuinely amazed that I've survived such a punishing schedule.

I am equally amazed when our editor at Virgin accepts such an incredibly long book, albeit that she makes me remove some material into appendices. They decide to give it the somewhat arrogant yet catchy title *Giza: The Truth*, and it's published in hardback in 1999. Of course the fabled 'Hall' wasn't discovered the previous year as Cayce had predicted, but that doesn't seem to detract from the fevered atmosphere that continues to surround the plateau in the run up to the new millennium. So initial sales are encouraging, and we undertake a number of talks at conferences and so on. The following year a slightly updated paperback version comes out. The book will go on to sell nearly 20,000 copies worldwide, which isn't bad for a debut.

In truth I'm nowhere near as fascinated by Giza as one might expect. I have written this book because it has provided a way into the industry – albeit that I've given it absolutely my best shot. But one major thing about the experience has stayed with me ever since, and continues to make me proud.

Given the foregoing descriptions it will perhaps come as no surprise that the book has come down heavily on the side of the scholarly, academic, Egyptian orthodoxy that best-selling writers like Hancock and Bauval love to bait and belittle. Indeed we've now presented them with a serious problem, because we've written a book supporting the orthodoxy, yet they can't indulge in their favourite tactic of accusing us of having a vested interest because we're part of it. We are not. We are completely independent researchers, and not even the most rabid conspiracy theorist can suggest otherwise.

Of course our work attracts an understandable mixture of praise and criticism. Because I'm new to this it takes time to get used to the more outlandish criticism, especially when it becomes personal rather than about the issues themselves. In time I will learn to either ignore unpleasant emails and reviews, or even better to respond to them with humour, but not yet. Nevertheless I want people to be able to see the correspondence between myself and the researchers whose work I'm critiquing, so I set up a website called the 'Giza: The Truth Discussion Site'. It continues to be available within the relevant section of my modern website, and still makes for interesting and sometimes hilarious reading.

The key point I take from all this, however, is this. Never, ever trust anything that you read without checking the primary sources for yourself. This is of course nothing more than the standard approach to good scholarship, but in the alternative world it's especially vital. So for me the real gift of my work on *Giza: The Truth* is that it teaches me to be far more discerning.

As an example, what are we to make of Hancock and Bauval's copious endnotes supporting their apparently hugely scholarly works? Sadly they're not worth the paper they're written on in some instances. Not that I'm suggesting for one moment their work is entirely worthless overall, far from it. But sometimes they go badly wrong, either through careless scholarship or, who knows, maybe they just like to muddy the water sometimes for effect? They wouldn't be the first authors to sex up their work to increase sales.

To be more specific, when I check some of their

references it turns out they're just copied from other authors' books, but when I finally trace them back to the primary source I find it's been completely misinterpreted or, worse still, deliberately distorted or even fabricated. A fine example of this is their suggestion that the Great Pyramid may be far older than Egyptologists think, which is put into their books almost as an afterthought. In this particular example the intermediate source they use is the supposedly great Sitchin, whose work so fascinated Sarah and I at the outset. But in fact his supposed evidence regarding the date of the Pyramid proves to be complete and utter bunkum when properly investigated.

More generally, it turns out that he's the worst offender of the lot in terms of his self-trumpeted scholarship. Correspondence with proper university professionals, who prefer not to sully themselves by criticising his work publicly, prove that he knows about as much about the intricacies of Sumerian and Akkadian scripts and grammar as I do. They provide me with concrete examples of his complete failure to appreciate the complexities of these scripts, often confusing and conflating them in his outlandish reinterpretations. His work is a hotchpotch of complete fabrication. About the best you can say is that if it was written as a novel it might make for a diverting read.

Having discovered this I spend considerable time preparing detailed papers on Sitchin's apparent scholarship, for example comparing his interpretations of texts to those of the academics, and publishing them on my website. It should come as no surprise that he provides precisely no proper references for his fantasies – which should have acted as a warning to me originally, but like so many of his readership I was too inexperienced and excited by his work to notice. This makes it hard to trace every supposed quote that he uses, but I persevere. Sometimes I find that he's omitted entire lines from the middle of passages which, if left in, would render his supposed interpretation absolutely contextually impossible.

That is why I can be absolutely certain that the man himself *knows* he's engaging in complete fabrication. I don't so much mind people just being stupid or unknowingly presenting inaccurate information, but to *deliberately* mislead is something else again – and is particularly disturbing because Sitchin is peddling the myth that the human race is completely under the control of the Anunnaki gods who genetically created us. In my opinion knowingly trying to take away our sense of self determination as a race is about as heinous a crime as anyone could possibly perpetrate, especially when he has a readership of millions around the world – and this is one of the few occasions in my life where I'm genuinely furious.

It is interesting to note that while he was still alive Sitchin was one of the most proactive litigators around, suing anyone who dared to criticise his work. I know he had heard about my website, but he never came near me.

He didn't dare.

While building up to writing *Giza: The Truth* I have also been undertaking much broader research into the idea that a lost Atlantean-style civilisation did indeed exist tens of thousands of years ago. But this has to be tempered with a little realism and discernment, as always. So I come to the conclusion that reports of advanced artefacts and modern human remains dating back *millions* of years again suffer from basic lack of scholarship. Also that any suggestion of advanced *technology* in this earlier civilisation is almost certainly wide of the mark.

For example, an artefact dubbed the 'Baghdad Battery' has been dated to several thousand years ago, and replicas have proved that when filled with acidic grape juice it would have been capable of producing a small but sufficient electric current to, for example, electroplate a silver statuette with gold. But if you only stop to think about the context there's absolutely no widespread evidence of the use of electricity either before or after this date. So, if it *is* what some say it is, the much more interesting question is how did we manage to discover electricity all that time ago but not make any further use of it for nearly two thousand years?

Rather more amusing is the story of the so-called 'Coso artefact', a supposedly anomalous geode found by three mineral hunters in California in 1961. When cut in half it revealed what appeared to be a replica of a modern spark plug – buried in a lump of rock dating back tens or even hundreds of thousands of years! But what those alternative researchers who continue to champion this find haven't bothered to find out is that subsequent investigation of x-rays has proved this to be no great surprise, because this wasn't an ancient geode at all but a recently formed conglomerate – and its supposedly enigmatic contents have now been matched perfectly to a plug made by the Champion Company in the 1920s.

So, rather than joining these wild goose chases, what really interest me are the consistent references in ancient texts from all around the world that talk of a highly spiritual race of people who somehow became debased and were wiped out by a major catastrophe. So I'm collating these into publishable form. From a physical point of view there's also extensive evidence of widespread flooding and destruction at the end of the last Ice Age. Some of this even suggests this may have been a sudden event caused by a major comet or asteroid impact that wiped out many species, and possibly a significant proportion of the human population too. But I'm also aware that there's evidence both for and against this last theory, and I intend to make that clear so I can't be accused of being selective and hypocritical.

I am on much stronger ground when reporting recent excavations by a Franco-Syrian team at Jerf el-Ahmar in Syria, which have pushed the date of Neolithic urbanization back as far as 11,500 years ago. I have been in communication with the head of that team, Danielle Stordeur, and she has kindly sent me a number of previously unpublished photographs. They show communal stone buildings on a significant scale, some with stone carvings on the walls, and even some evidence of prototype pictographic writing – all this accompanied by evidence of crop cultivation and domestication of grain. Unfortunately Jerf and other nearby sites have already been submerged by the construction of new dams in the area, but at least their existence has been properly documented.

This level of sophistication cannot spring suddenly from nowhere, there have to be precedents. My growing suspicion is that this is evidence of a previous civilisation who were *culturally* rather than technologically advanced, and who managed to save themselves by somehow predicting the upcoming disaster and the tsunamis that would obliterate their coastal settlements – coastal because I suspect they were almost certainly trading far and wide via boat. It seems reasonable to suggest they would have escaped to high ground inland, and the widespread Syrian settlements would then represent the start of the rebuilding process.

The corollary is that they may not have built in stone or even used ceramics previously, because wood and other materials would do just as well, particularly in mild climates. But while these materials could provide a perfectly sophisticated standard of living, they are of course biodegradable and would leave no archaeological trace – especially after any settlements had been submerged by worldwide sea level rises. Subsequently, when it came to rebuilding and protecting themselves from less civilised survivors, stone structures would have become more of a necessity.

I put all this into a book called *Genesis Unveiled*, but initially Virgin don't want to know. I even have to self-publish on CD as a stopgap, because I've been promising the book to avid supporters of my work for a while.

By now I've also sold my cottage in Hamble. The

money I'd put by from my consultancy days ran out so I needed to liquidate some capital. In late 2001 I use the profit to invest in a beautiful 40-foot Trader, a fibreglass-hulled motor boat with a largely wooden superstructure that resembles a classical fishing vessel. It is emphatically *not* your typical, modern 'plastic palace', and nor have I bought it as a toy – I'll be living on it.

Initially I stay in marinas on the Hamble River, and I take all the necessary qualifications – although learning to navigate and moor a boat of that size on such a tricky and highly tidal river is a real challenge. But this is the most expensive area in the country for moorings, whereas I'm supposed to be living as frugally as possible. So one day I take a day trip to Brighton and I'm amazed at how cheap the berths are in its huge marina on the edge of such a wonderful town. They have space too, and I'm there like a shot.

Not long after this I realise I'm going to have to do some sort of work to bring some money in, so I invest in the regulation white van and sign up with a small, local courier company. In no time I'm their lead driver – the only real requirement is reliability – but making a profit is tough, and often I'm living from week to week and from hand to mouth. On one of my longer jobs I find I have just enough money for diesel to get me to Newcastle and back, and I have a packet of tobacco for roll-ups, but nothing more with which to buy food. Still, it keeps me slim!

By the end of 2002 I'm still not earning enough and I know I need to sell the boat to liquidate some more capital. I am ok with this because I'm fully committed to my fledgling writing career. The trouble is it will be much easier to sell back in Hamble, but Brighton Marina won't let me leave because I owe several months rent. As a guarantee I offer to let them keep my rib, which is worth way more than what I owe them, but they're having none of it.

Eventually I have to recruit one of my closest mates from my bike racing days, Chris 'Wingnut' McGahan, to help me break out early one morning. The trouble is I stupidly haven't checked that the engines will start, and of course at 5am they decide they're not in the mood. We wait 'til the chandlery is open to buy some 'fast start' to spray into the intakes, but by now it's broad daylight. Nevertheless no one challenges us as we motor past the marina entrance and on up the coast. The only real problem comes when Chris warns me he thinks we're a little too close into shore.

'Rubbish!' I say, 'I've got all the charts out, I'm on the right heading, I know what I'm doing.' And in my head I'm thinking, 'I'm the captain of this vessel matey, so don't you start pushing your weight around.'

'So why's the depth gauge plummeting, and a bloke standing on that sandbank just off our starboard side?' The bastard even uses the correct language. I fling the wheel to the left. I have forgotten to adjust for the tide, but at least I've provided Chris with an anecdote he can use again – and again, and again.

Not long after the move back a change at Virgin provides me with an opening in the form of a new sales director, apparently a former car dealer from the East End. After continual badgering my editor tells me she's prepared to resubmit *Genesis Unveiled* to him provided I prepare a synopsis in which all references to spirituality are removed. I comply and wait with bated breath, although by now I've started to come across the idea of conscious creation and manifestation enough that I'm regularly imagining scenarios and chanting mantras connected with success in this scenario

On the appointed afternoon she phones and, with much hilarity, impersonates his exact words from the editorial meeting: ‘S’pose ‘is first one done alright, might as well ‘ave a gamble on this one too.’ After all our effort on the synopsis it takes around twenty seconds for the decision to be made. No further discussion required.

The book is published in hardback late in 2003, and initially sales are very poor. It looks like it will be a complete failure until hard work by Virgin leads to a significant article in the *Daily Mail* that saves the day. It comes out in paperback the following year and will eventually sell over 10,000 copies.

Around this time I’m also instrumental in setting up the ‘Group With No Name’, a focal point for alternative authors and researchers with like minds and similar interests. We meet once a month, usually in a room above one of the pubs in Bloomsbury. We are all good friends, and with people of the calibre of Clive Prince, Lynn Picknett and Andrew Collins our discussions are lively and pretty well-informed. We all gain benefit from being able to bounce ideas off each other, share contacts and so on.

So what of Sarah and me? Well, not long after she moved in she started a brief affair with a work colleague – clearly a case of once she'd got what she'd chased for so long she became easily bored. But I forgave her and she then moved in properly. We lived together while I was writing *Giza: The Truth* but tensions were increasing and, when she finally told me that a large angel kept appearing in the bedroom doorway and telling her she had to leave me, the writing was on the wall. To this day I've no idea whether she really believed we'd lived together in Atlantis or not, but in retrospect it's clear we were never really suited as romantic partners. Yet it was her and no one else who put me on the path I've trodden ever since – and for that, despite all its ups and downs, I will be eternally grateful.

Was it just chance that I met her? I don't think so. The desire to go and talk to her that first day was just too strong and had no obvious explanation. Just what it was that brought us together we'll find out in due course.

2004

an uncomfortable past

I am lying on the couch of one of Britain's leading practitioners of hypnotic regression. His name is Andy Tomlinson, and he's going to attempt to take me back in time. Way back in time. Not just to my childhood, but beyond even that, back into a *past* life. I figure that, because I'm just about to write a book about such things, I'd better try to experience one for myself. Neither of us knows where or how this will go and, never having done it before, I'm not even sure if I'll make a good subject. But here we go anyway.

After the initial hypnosis he starts with some questions about what I'm wearing to 'ground' me in this other life. I report tights and new-ish black shoes with buckles; green, billowy trousers with gold stripes; a matching jacket with billowy arms; and underneath a white shirt. We then establish that I'm a man in his late twenties to early thirties, and I'm standing alone in the central market area of a town in daytime. As to my feelings I initially report being quite proud, even arrogant.

I have some sort of official capacity that involves reading a document to the people in the market. Andy has to push me to establish that I'm laying down a list of rules or similar, the penalty for breaking them being severe – torture or death. The location is somewhere in Spain, and the infamous 'Inquisition' is just getting underway. Yet underneath all the pomp I'm very much in two minds about what's going on.

We jump to the next major incident in this life. I declare that I'm 'in the shit' because 'I've finally denounced what's been going on'. I evince a reluctance to go into this part of the experience, but Andy gently pushes me. He knows what he's doing and he'll make sure any emotional issues that arise are healed and dealt with. From now on I'll quote direct from the transcript, with ellipses' representing Andy's questions and other bits I've omitted for conciseness.

> I'm in a cell. And I can hear other people being tortured and stuff. I know that's going to happen to me as well… I think I've been here for a little while. I've already been roughed up a bit… It's worse for me because I was in authority before and helped to bring it all in, so for me to stand up now is much worse for them… They're going to be that much harder about trying to get me to retract… So I'm scared shitless at the moment. But I also know

that I've got to do what's right.

I can hear them coming down the corridor. The keys jangling... They're all wearing uniforms... Some sort of dark blue tops and white trousers... There's one on each side of me, one ahead, and a couple behind... I'm handcuffed. I think my feet might be shackled as well, they're dragging a bit.

(Big sigh) To start with they take me to see the people who are in charge of the whole thing... There's one serious one. He's got all his Catholic regalia on. Purple I think. Lots of big chains and crosses, some big high ruff collar I think, something like that... I think they're trying to argue with me intellectually, to make out that I'm being stupid. I know that I have to defend my position, and it's a much easier one to defend than theirs is, from an intellectual point of view. So that's what I do, and it's not very difficult... They're very upset because I'm making them look a little bit foolish so they don't like it... They get rid of me as quick as they can.

We all know what's going to happen to me... I think they're going to give me another night in

> the cell just to think about it, and get very scared about it, that's their way... I'm still scared shitless but I know that I've got to do the right thing. I'm praying for strength.

Andy directs me to move on to what happens the next morning.

> I haven't slept. I think they've got me chained to the wall anyway... They're taking me to where all the equipment is... (Sighing throughout) Racks... There's clamps for holding your hands so they can pull your fingernails out, and toenails... What I don't know is how long they're going to try and do this for, how long I'm going to be conscious, and how many days I might have to put up with this for.

Again I'm reluctant to go further so Andy instructs me that only the memories will come through, not the emotions and bodily sensations. This particularly because our main aim here is research rather than therapy. He asks me how they start and, despite the protection, my answers are heavily punctuated with deep sighs.

> The nails, the fingernails... Left hand... I think

> the first time they did the whole hand, without even stopping, one by one, because they know damn well you're not going to give in just after that first one, even though it hurts like hell. After the first hand is finished, they give you the chance to say something. [On the next hand] they do two or three, and ask, and then the last couple.

Andy moves me on to the next torture session, this time involving the rack.

> The table's in two halves, and they rotate a wheel to pull the two halves apart... When you pass out they throw a bucket of water over you, and do it again... [This happened] at least two or three times... I think I must have come round back in the cell again. Whatever else they did after that, I'm not sure I want to remember it. I just know it wasn't good... (Slightly incoherent) It didn't go on for weeks, thank god, but it must have been days, I guess... It seemed like an eternity.

Finally he directs me to the point just before I take my last breath.

> I hardly know who or what I am any more. I've been knocked around so much. My body's just

> broken, completely a ruin... I'm just so grateful it's all going to be over, and that I've held firm... Of course I want to die! I don't want to carry on going through this any more... I think they're doing something to me but they've just stopped, and I know I'm going to go now.

We go through a variety of healing exercises at the end of the session, just to make sure nothing unpleasant will stay with me.

Of course after this experience my head is full of questions going round and round. Does it *prove* that I've lived before? Not in the slightest. Could it easily have been assembled in my subconscious, from my imagination and from historical information I already possessed? Of course. There are no real details in there that I wouldn't have already known, and there may even be some aspects that an expert on the Spanish Inquisition – which I'm not – would be able to spot as incorrect. Given that I also come out of it as a bit of a hero, was it all just a big ego trip? Possibly. Having said that, in due course I'll be regressed into many other lives that aren't heroic or noteworthy at all.

Was I genuinely in trance? Yes, because

although I was sufficiently conscious throughout that I remember what happened, it took some hours for me to return to normal. Did Andy effectively make the story up for me with his questioning? Admittedly most of the session was led by him, but maybe that was mainly because I wasn't a particularly good subject and needed plenty of prompting to remember things. More telling is that on a few occasions I even contradicted him when he appeared to be leading me in the wrong direction.

For now I come to the conclusion that, on balance, this was a genuine past life. It certainly *felt* real.

To understand why I was in Andy's therapy room, we need to step back in time a bit. We have seen that meeting Sarah in 1996 was the *first* 'shock' to my spiritual system, in that she was the catalyst for me to start thinking about issues such as intuition and so on. But the second shock took its time, not arriving until early 2003.

Virgin had received the first draft manuscript of *Genesis Unveiled*. As usual for me it was way too long and needed huge swathes cutting out and putting onto my website or into appendices. But more to the point I was already talking about basic spiritual ideas such as soul survival, reincarnation and karma, having discussed these with Sarah too. I was using the argument that our 'forgotten race' of ancestors had been wiped out by an essentially karmic catastrophe because of their increasing departure from spiritual ways – remember this was the main theme of all the ancient texts. I was also suggesting there was strong *evidence* for these basic spiritual ideas. My editor's reaction was, 'You never explain what this evidence you're referring to is!'

So I set about collating it properly. For some time I'd been familiar with the pioneering research of Professor Ian Stevenson of the University of Virginia into children who remember past lives, undertaken since the early 1960s. His scholarly, evidential approach to spirituality resonated with me hugely. Although by now I was learning to meditate, to trust my intuition and to be always on the look out for important synchronicities that might push me in a certain direction, this was as far as my personal journey had taken me. I wasn't especially telepathic, mediumistic or anything else, and unlike many people I didn't feel I needed personal experience to 'believe'. Instead this kind of evidential approach felt right for me.

But in broadening my search after the request from Virgin I stumbled across the equally pioneering regression evidence of his fellow countryman Michael Newton. Rather than just taking people back into their past lives, he was concentrating on recall of their time *between* lives, or 'interlife' as I'd later call it. This was the *second* shock to my spiritual system, because I found his subjects' testimony incredibly compelling in its apparent consistency. All of a sudden everything in my developing worldview made sense.

It ran as follows. We live many lives to experience all sides of the coin. Then in the interlife we review the life just lived to see what we did well and what not so well, although there's no judgment by an all-seeing deity or any other spiritual hierarchy. Instead we're our *own* harshest critics. Most stunning of all for me was an idea I'd only seen hinted at once and then only briefly, in *The Celestine Prophecy*. It was that we're closely involved in *choosing and planning our own next life*, and the challenges it will present us with so we can hopefully overcome them and grow.

This more than anything was what really blew me away, because it resonated so strongly. So we really did have to take personal responsibility for everything about our lives, just as I'd concluded at school – but from a purely Earthly perspective. There was no 'God's will' or 'judgment from on high'. We might get help and advice from various guides and so on, but basically we each run our own show. This was a huge turning point for me.

But when *Genesis Unveiled* came out that summer, although it sold well after the *Daily Mail* article, I was somewhat disappointed that readers seemed far more interested in the exposure I gave to Newton's work than they were in my own ideas about the forgotten race. So much so that for some months I was unsure where to go next with my fledgling writing career – if I went anywhere at all.

I had a real choice to make. Should I risk all on one last throw of the dice, and write again? Or give it up and do something 'sensible', as so many well-meaning friends advised? The answer would depend entirely on whether anything came up that I felt was worth the risk. It had to be something important enough that it would effectively leave me with no choice. I have always maintained that I'm not really a writer in that I don't feel the compunction to write all the time, only when I think I've got something important to say.

Early in 2004 I decided to take a two-week holiday in Cancun, partly justifying it on the basis that at last I would get to see some of the Mayan pyramids in the Yucatan about which I'd heard and read so much. It was here that everything became suddenly clear. I would sit on the balcony of my hotel room and immerse myself in the view: a pristine stretch of pure white sand, bordered by a translucent sea whose hues graduated through every shade of turquoise before turning the deepest blue. I had never seen anything so beautiful or transfixing.

But I would also read. I had been gradually picking up leads about other pioneering regression therapists who'd undertaken interlife research, and I took along several such books, some of which were hard to source. To my surprise and delight it turned out they were all saying the same basic things about life reviews, life planning and so on! So I suddenly realised that unearthing all the interlife pioneers and comparing their findings would be an important and as yet unexplored piece of research.

The thing that resonated with me most was that all this was *not* based on sacred texts from thousands of years ago, or on the dictates of some prophet or guru, but on the testimony of hundreds if not thousands of ordinary people. I would never look at life the same way again. I resolved that I'd always try to analyse any situation not so much from a human but from a *soul* perspective.

Nor was that all. For some time I'd been considering the whole issue of a more evidence-based approach to spirituality. I had already written a magazine article entitled 'Spiritual Rationalism' at the end of 2003, but now I swapped the words around because it flowed better. What's more I determined to write a whole new book containing all the evidence for 'Rational Spirituality' I could unearth.

This meant putting the interlife to one side for a moment and concentrating on more basic evidence of soul survival and of past lives. I decided there were three areas of research that best fitted the bill: near-death experiences, children who spontaneously remember past lives, and adult recall of past lives via regression.

Stepping back for one moment, what led me to believe in the survival of the soul after death in the first place? During my discussions with Sarah I can remember coming across an explanation that likened our consciousness to a television or radio transmitter and the brain to an aerial that picks up the signal – so even if the aerial is destroyed the transmitter continues to broadcast. I really resonated with that metaphor. But, rather than let this just remain a *belief*, my research now uncovered compelling *evidence* in the form of a number of near-death experience cases that strongly pointed towards consciousness existing independently of the physical body and brain.

One involved a woman remembering details of an operation to remove an aneurysm from her brain, which at the time had been deliberately cooled so that she was clinically dead. These details – such as the shape of the saw used, and a conversation that occurred between the surgeon and one of the nurses – weren't only subsequently verified, but also could only have been picked up while her brain was completely dormant.

Another involved a Russian neuroscientist and devout atheist who was run over by the KGB to prevent him from going to work in the US. He lay in a morgue for three days before someone noticed a twitch, but when he came round he described having travelled around out of his body, including to another part of the hospital where a newborn baby wouldn't stop crying. In his nonphysical state he was able to detect a greenstick fracture of the hip, which the doctors subsequently confirmed.

Meanwhile the most compelling cases of past-life regression were provided by Peter Ramster, an Australian psychologist hardly known in the UK until I started making widespread references to his work. In the early 1980s he brought four of his best regression subjects over to Europe to check out their memories of past lives in Britain, France and Germany, and the results, as revealed in his documentary *The Reincarnation*

Experiments, were spectacular. The facts they'd remembered in trance back in their homeland weren't only subsequently verified over here, but also *so incredibly obscure* as to be most logically explained by paranormal rather than normal mechanisms. In fact this is the key evidential 'acid test' that must always be applied in all these fields of research.

By way of example, one woman remembered studying medicine at the University of Aberdeen in the 1830s, and was able to describe and sketch both the interior and exterior of Marischal College as it was at the time. Much of what she had drawn and remembered was confirmed when they visited, accompanied by a local historian and a local journalist. But some details seemed wrong when compared to the earliest pictures and drawings they had access to. Remember that like most buildings this one had changed a great deal over time. So was she wrong, or had there been earlier changes?

This question was resolved when a local man who had written an unpublished postgraduate paper on the history of the building was consulted – and all the details were confirmed. He even quizzed her about how one would have got from Point A to Point B in the interior of the original building, and was stunned by the accuracy of her answers. The only copy of his paper was in the Open University archives, and it's almost inconceivable that Ramster's subject could have gained access to this with the deliberate intention of perpetrating an elaborate fraud. Not only that but she remembered other obscure details about the doctor's hometown of Blairgowrie.

The boat sells early in 2004, and I've got money in the bank again even after paying off my debts. This includes what I owe to Brighton Marina – I don't want you thinking I'm a man of no integrity – as well as to my sister Christine. She runs a very successful women's clothes shop in Southampton, alongside her husband David's men's version, and very kindly gave me a loan some time ago when things were tight.

Nevertheless to try to keep my living expenses down I start renting a room in a house shared with my nephew Mike in a less than salubrious area of Southampton. My combined bedroom and office lies next to the dividing wall of the other half of our semidetached house, which is occupied by probably the most psychotic family on the planet. They are all female and the mother is a highly active drug dealer, so people are arriving at all hours of the day and night. But the situation doesn't need other people to make it almost unbearable.

Have you ever tried to distil some of the finer points of the meaning of life while being bombarded with loud urban music at all hours of the day and night? Or by vicious arguments so punctuated by swear words that there's very little room left for anything else? None of this is helped by the fact it's a hot summer and it's impossible not to open my window, which looks directly onto their back garden. Since previous attempts to complain about the noise have all met with threats and scratched cars, it seems that the only option is to grin and bear it. Which is what I do, even if at times I think I might go completely mad.

In the interim I approach Virgin to see if they're interested in publishing the book I've provisionally called *Interlife*. I guess I should be appreciative that they're keen to work with me again – but only if I write another history-cum-archaeology book. After my experience with *Genesis Unveiled*, perhaps it should come as no surprise that they feel completely unable to take a book that's so clearly focused on spiritual issues alone. The synopsis is also rejected by several other publishers. So do I have the determination to carry on, and again complete a book without having a publishing deal already signed and sealed?

I do, and I am I think justifiably proud when the first draft is finished after only six months of intense writing and research – especially under such extreme and trying conditions. Never let anyone tell you that they've got 'writer's block', or can only write in a special place or whatever. If you're motivated enough, you can write literally *anywhere*, and under any circumstances.

The trouble is it turns out that the hardest part is *still* yet to come. I begin my final read-through with some anticipation that within days all will be complete. It starts well. But halfway through I arrive at the chapter that concerns the dynamics of karma, and here I get stuck. It is very unusual for me to have to make significant amendments to my work after a first draft, because a great deal of thought goes into that initial effort. But here I am rewriting the first half of that chapter again, and again, and again. Each time thinking I have solved the problem, only to go back again and realise I haven't. I just don't seem to be able to find any clarity about certain discrepancies in the modern research. So even when my 'eureka' moment does finally arrive, I have no great confidence that I've actually cracked it.

But a few days' break with my racing friend Chris in the Isle of Man does the trick, and when I return refreshed I realise that my fears are groundless. What I thought might read like the ramblings of a deluded idiot finally makes some sense. In a nutshell I conclude that whatever karmic dynamics shape our lives they have little to do with some sort of punishment for supposed wrongs in past lives, and far more to do with gaining *experience*, and seeing how we deal with different challenges across different lives.

As a prime example of this – although I have to be sensitive about how I put it across – people with physical or mental disabilities almost certainly aren't being punished for some past misdeed at all, as more traditional Eastern approaches would have us believe. Instead it is much more likely they've chosen their circumstances before birth to really stretch themselves and experience far more potential for growth than someone having it easy. Often, too, they're altruistically providing a magnificent example to the rest of us.

With this final piece of the jigsaw in place I have no alternative but to press ahead with the courage of my own convictions, set up 'Rational Spirituality Press', and publish the book myself. What is more, just for good measure, I decide to change the title to *The Book of the Soul*.

I believe very strongly in this idea of Rational Spirituality that I'm putting across in the book. One of my major objectives is to show that you can hold a spiritual worldview *and* still have your feet planted firmly on the ground. This is important because, even if interest in orthodox religion has been steadily waning in the Western world, I'm convinced that our increasingly affluent and materialistic lifestyles are still leaving many of us feeling deeply unfulfilled.

So for me it's vital that ordinary people, who

sense there must be something more to life but are alienated by the dogma of many orthodox religions, aren't put off their own spiritual exploration through fear of turning themselves into a 'new age' laughing stock. I strongly believe it doesn't *have* to be like that and, while the new age movement has been invaluable, my feeling is that it's now time for us to move forward and bring proper, grounded spirituality into the mainstream of Western thought.

There is another crucial aspect of all this. From about the middle of the last century intellectual culture in the West has tended to be dominated by 'materialists' – that is, people who regard all religion as bunkum, maintaining that the physical, *material* world is all there is. They often do this for understandable reasons – for example they've seen the damage that religious belief can do, and the wars and other conflicts that have been propagated in its name for millennia. They understand that this is far more often about the human politics of power than about religion per se. But they also find the fundamental beliefs inherent in all religions entirely illogical – just as I once did.

The mistake this intellectual elite make is to

conflate a more broadly based spirituality with religious belief, thereby 'throwing the baby out with the bathwater'. For intellectuals ranging from biologist Richard Dawkins to media darling Stephen Fry, any worldview perceived to be based on belief and faith is illogical – and the barely veiled insinuation is that any holders thereof are possessed of the intellectual capacity of an amoeba. Whereas I hold the strong belief that this is demonstrably wrong – and that it's high time the materialist establishment was shaken out of this smug complacency and given a bloody nose.

In fact I'd go as far as to argue that, in the face of modern scientific and other evidence, a broad spiritual worldview provides a far more logical and philosophical framework for understanding the universe than a materialist one – indeed that it's the far more *rational* position to adopt. This is why Rational Spirituality uses the strap line 'evidence not faith'.

It is with this strength of conviction that, perhaps somewhat foolishly, Liz and I set up what we call the Rational Spirituality Movement. She is eighteen years my junior and lives with her two young girls in Southend in Essex. We meet at a party hosted by my writer friend Andrew Collins, and that night she tells his wife that at last she has met the man of her dreams. As for me I'm initially not sure about a girl who is so skinny she looks anorexic – although it turns out that she eats like a horse when she wants to. But I'm captivated by her vivacity, intelligence and cutting – if sometimes quite earthy – wit. She is also strongly into spirituality of the type I'm espousing.

Never one to do anything by halves, that night she intimates she would like me to move up to Southend to be with her. For my part I need a change and have been waiting for an excuse to get away from Southampton for some time anyway. I have also been single for some time, and Liz is the first girl that has properly captured my attention. So within six weeks I find myself moving myself up to Southend and into a flat Liz has just rented. Every morning I'm now woken early by two young girls, Jess aged three and Gracie aged five, jumping all over the bed and wanting to play. As someone who has only rarely lived with a partner before, and certainly not one with small children, this is completely alien... and I love it.

I guess it won't be honest unless I admit that Liz is quite recently married when I meet her, and living with her husband. In fact he was even at the party, but without wishing to be disrespectful they seemed so mismatched, and talked to each other so little, that it was quite some time before I even realised they were together. It was a difficult situation to be sure, but Liz was convinced she was doing the right thing leaving John, so I went with it.

In fact he lives just round the corner, and is so incredibly mature about the whole thing that within a few months we're having a beer together in the local discussing Rational Spirituality. He gives no sign that his heart must be breaking, because it's now abundantly clear to me just how much he loves Liz and the girls. John himself would admit that he's not the most prepossessing man to look at, but in terms of humility and integrity you'd have to go a very, very long way to find a better.

In any case, piggybacking off sales of *The Book of the Soul*, the Rational Spirituality Movement attracts several hundred followers in just a few months. I even put together a list of ten precepts, which to me aren't things to *believe* in, but a sensible way to look at life based on the evidence. I set up a PO Box and at one point I find therein a completely anonymous donation of £500 – accompanied only by the message 'from little acorns mighty oaks grow'. Liz and I are incredibly touched, and put the money towards a video camera for the new book I'm working on. Which I guess I'd better talk about.

At an exhibition where we have a stall selling my book I'm approached by a man who makes small talk for a while before revealing that he takes pictures of ghosts. He even takes a few out of his bag and they look fairly impressive. Although I'm relatively new as a writer, I still realise that there are quite a few rather disturbed people around who engage in all sorts of fantasies, and I'm always a little wary while trying to remain a decent and trusting human being. But neither Liz nor I get any sort of bad vibe from Ron, so when he says he wants me to write a book containing his photos I agree to get back to him in a few days.

When I do I make it abundantly clear that if we're to work together I'll have to seriously put him to the test, because I need to know he's not a hoaxer, not least because I have my own reputation to protect. On the other hand if his pictures are genuine they're undoubtedly the best collection there's ever been. I tell him that I'll need to go out with him at night with a video camera to record everything he's doing, and that I'll also need to provide the digital memory card for his own camera – which I will insert at the beginning of the night and then take away at the end, to preclude any possibility of him tampering with the images. He agrees with no hesitation whatsoever.

Our first trip takes us to a ruined church in rural Essex that had suffered a fire. As soon as we enter the front gate around midnight we hear a sudden noise overhead and Ron nearly jumps out of his skin – as a couple of birds fly out of a tree. Not a good sign from a supposed ghost hunter. I am not the bravest guy in the world but, just as with my claustrophobia in the Pyramid, I'm here to do a job.

We do two more site visits after this. One is to a country pub whose landlady is none too happy to accommodate us. Although we all notice an incredibly strong smell of lavender at the bottom of some stairs that lead to the supposedly most haunted room at the top, for which she has no explanation, Ron's photos from these trips stubbornly refuse to show anything abnormal at all. He says he can't understand it and, of course, shows me a couple of others he's taken in the meantime at other sites when I've not been there. Meanwhile I've sent a sample of his best photos to various professionals, including one often used as an expert witness in criminal trials, and none of them can find anything to suggest fraud.

Then, as I'm preparing a synopsis for potential publishers and putting a border around one of these best images, I notice it has an inexplicable white line running across the bottom. I can make no sense of what it might represent, so I call Ron and he insists it's a torch beam. I experiment with same in a darkened room with a flash camera and cannot replicate the effect at all, and now I'm seriously concerned. It looks as though an original picture has just been badly scanned so that the white area remains at the bottom.

Then Liz reminds me that her brother-in-law is a keen amateur photographer, so I send him some samples. In no time he comes back with a detailed report, explaining exactly how each one has been created. On extreme magnification several show the obvious signs of hairs and dust on the screen of a scanner, which he must have used to create some of them. With others he explains how, for example, careful application of a drop of water to a film-based photo can produce a blurred image. And so on and so forth.

Although we already had a strong sense that all was not well, we're still absolutely gobsmacked, more by the audacity of the man than anything else. I am furious, not least because by now he's wasted hundreds of hours of my time and, arguably worse, was prepared to jeopardise my reputation despite all my warnings. Thank heaven we've found out he's a fraud before I've gone any further with potential publishers.

I call him. He seems to take it all very calmly, and I have no idea what to make of him. A part of me feels sorry for him – it's almost as if he so wants what he does to be true that he convinces himself it *is* true, and is able to dismiss his fakery from his consciousness. I tell him I will take no further action myself unless I hear that he's touting his pictures to others, in which case I'll step in very publicly.

In retrospect I guess it's rather funny that he was able to take me on such a wild *ghost* chase.

Andy and I get to know each other better during this time, not least because Liz enrols with his new Past Life Regression Academy. But it's a pleasant surprise when towards the end of 2005 he asks if I'd like to write a book with him. Initially he wants it be about interlife regression generally, based on his extensive client history, but of course it's not long before I'm expanding the remit. What if he chooses say ten of his best subjects, puts them into deep trance so they enter the interlife, asks them a series of preplanned questions, then we compare their answers for consistency? Would that not be something that hadn't been attempted before?

Andy is taken by the idea and, while he selects and approaches his chosen subjects, I start to put a first draft of the questions together. They cover everything from trapped spirits to demonic beings, from the purpose of incarnation to life on other planets, from legends of Atlantis to the future of humanity, and from multiple realities to the true nature of time. I also prepare a questionnaire for the chosen subjects asking them about relevant books they may have read – for example by Newton or any of the other interlife pioneers, or even by myself – and about general levels of interest in some of the other areas, such as human prehistory and so on.

The sessions themselves take nearly a year to complete, not least because some subjects need several to complete the questions. But then the real work of editing begins. I have already been selecting and editing the standard interlife sessions I want to use for the first part of the book, which is in itself no mean feat. But the new sessions require even more work. There is a lot of commonality in the answers, but there are many discrepancies too, and deciding which bits to edit out – as being perhaps unduly influenced by prior knowledge, or by Andy's questions and so on – is a serious challenge. All this despite the questionnaire replies revealing relatively little prior knowledge amongst most of the subjects, while Andy has done what he can to keep any 'leading' questions to a minimum.

In any case it's certainly an interesting piece of work, and once it's complete it's time to publish.

This time we've already had an offer from Hay House, a well-known publishing company that specialises in mind-body-spirit books, but just before we sign the contract I ask how many words we should be working towards. They tell me it's 75k, and that it must be exactly that, no more, no less. I have already got around 100k words and the book is only three quarters complete. It is going to be impossible, given the nature of the material, to comply with their demands.

I offer to send them a trial chapter so they can show me how they might edit the book down, but they've lost interest. To them I'm now just a 'problem author' and it's time to move on to the next one. I am incredibly annoyed, but given time I come to realise that because the publishing industry generally is already struggling they simply have to do what they think is right to succeed. In the meantime the book has been turned down by other potential publishers, so Andy and I are on our own again.

What is more he and I are now having something of a disagreement too about how the book should be presented. I have a certain style when I'm writing one of my more scholarly books or articles, and I don't want to compromise that. Andy thinks a more relaxed style is appropriate. We compromise by splitting the book in two. He publishes the first part about the interlife generally under the title *Exploring the Eternal Soul*, having made any editorial changes he sees fit, while I publish the new research of the second part as *The Wisdom of the Soul*. Both books are well received in the regression community, but don't necessarily make much of a wider impact.

Nevertheless, it's while writing this book that I come up with what I feel to be an excellent solution to an age-old conundrum. Basically spiritual people tend to fall into two groups. One sees our souls as individual entities, although acknowledging that there's also some sort of universal 'Source' – what some people might characterise as 'God' – from which we all sprang and with which we'll all ultimately reunite. The other regards any notion of the individuality of souls as an illusion, insisting that in fact we're 'all one' and that only the universal Source exists.

My suggestion is that, as so often with some of the more complex metaphysical ideas we struggle with, *both* are likely to be true at the same time – and that the concept of the hologram can usefully show us how. The definition of the 'holographic soul' that I come up with runs as follows:

> Soul consciousness is holographic. We are both individual aspects of Source, and full holographic representations of it, all at the same time. However this does not mean that soul individuality is in itself an illusion. The principle of the hologram is that the part contains the whole, and yet is clearly distinguishable from it.

What I don't recognise at the time is just how much spiritual power this confers on each of us as individual creator gods – and how crucial this will come to be in my future model of Supersoul Spirituality.

Towards the end of 2006 Andy is kind enough to introduce me to the company for whom he works as a part-time trainer, Parity. He knows my savings from the sale of the boat have run out and that financially life is a struggle for Liz and me. He also knows I used to manage IT projects back in the day, just as he did, so like him I should be able to train people in the highly popular PRINCE2 project management methodology, which is government backed. I attend two courses, one where he's the highly capable instructor, pass my exams, co-train alongside qualified colleagues on a couple more courses, then I'm good to go.

The earnings are terrific, and once more we can look forward to a decent life. Having been out of the game for more than a decade I never dreamed I'd be able to get a 'proper' job again. Plus I'm self-employed, the job doesn't have all the pressures of being an actual project manager any more, and I don't work full time so I still have the opportunity to write and research.

The following New Year we move into a rented flat right on the Esplanade in Southend, and life is really looking up. By the middle of the year I decide it would be a good idea to write a really simple 'pocket' book to explain Rational Spirituality for a broader audience. *The Little Book of the Soul* is duly born, and I spend some time selecting some of the best cases of near-death experience, children who remember past lives and past-life regression. I write them more in a story format, interspersed with my own simplified commentary about what we can infer from them.

I also decide that the way to market this book is to sell it via my website in batches of ten, at cost, so for £1 per copy. The idea is to encourage people to keep one copy and distribute the rest to friends and family, thus spreading the word. I don't need to profit from these books at the moment because I have well-paid work again – and in any case I'm hoping this will leverage sales of my other books.

Most important of all I once again appear on the well-known US radio show 'Coast to Coast AM', hosted by George Noory. It is on late at night in the US, so attracts its fair share of fruitcakes to the phone-in, plus you have to be up at silly o'clock in the morning UK time. But it's one of the few programmes or magazines that nearly always guarantees good sales as a result.

Having said that even I don't anticipate what follows. I am so excited I nearly faint when I see the first huge batch of orders on my computer screen. Within a six-week period I sell the entire

2000-copy initial print run and am into a reprint. I am flat out every day packing and posting off books. I really think that at last my prayers have been answered and my writing career will finally take off. Sadly this proves to be a false dawn. It isn't long before sales slow to a trickle. Nor has there been any significant increase in sales of my more serious books. I am pretty much back to square one, and a part of me almost wishes I hadn't been able to get my hopes up.

Not only that but, for Liz and me, a storm has been brewing for some time. When I first met her she didn't tell me she'd been on medication for depression since she was sixteen. Nor did she tell me she'd stopped taking the tablets as soon as we met. Nor was I aware that it takes about six weeks for the medication to completely work through the system – meaning that literally as I moved in I was confronted by a very different girl from the one I'd met and fallen for.

I felt I was committed, especially since two young girls were involved, so despite some horrendous rows even in the early weeks I stuck it out. What is more we did have a great many terrific times together. I loved the children and I loved Liz, and had never been so happy as when we all used to drive along in my old convertible jeep with the roof down singing Andy Williams' 'Beautiful Balloon' at the tops of our voices. On top of that she was seriously bright and we worked well together from the perspective of my writing and research – it was the first time since Sarah I'd had someone to bounce ideas off who understood what the hell I was on about.

Nevertheless we continued to have problems and rows off and on, and particularly after our move to the Esplanade I started to seriously question if I could carry on. Heaven knows I'm probably not the easiest person in the world to live with, although not for all the usual reasons – having lived on my own for many years I'm very housetrained, and don't leave dirty socks, pants and wet towels all over the place. But it's seriously wearing to wake up next to a person knowing that their first words will often be something like, 'I don't really want to wake up today, I can't see the point of it all.'

In the end, not long after I start *The Little Book of the Soul*, one particular disagreement ends with me telling Liz I've had enough. Initially she doesn't take it well. Although I immediately arrange to rent a flat on the other side of Southend so I can still be there for the girls, on one occasion I come home to find my office has been trashed.

Nevertheless after I move out things calm down, and for a while we're good friends and everything is better than it's been for a long time. In fact, after some cosmetic surgery that she has wanted for a long time and I help to finance, she becomes so much like the girl I once knew that I start to fall for her again. But by this time she's met someone else and, I guess understandably given her previous hurt, starts to play one off against the other. As soon as I hear little Jess talking about how he's coming round just after I leave, and how much she's looking forward to seeing him, it breaks my heart – although probably not one thousandth of how John's heart must have been broken when I put him in the same boat.

When I hear that the new man is moving in, and even that they're planning to have a child together, I realise the two girls will now have three dads: John, him and me. That is too many. One of us has to go and, no matter how much I'm going to miss them, it clearly has to be me.

With Liz and I falling out badly before I leave, and her family being so bitter about the whole thing that they've already been turning the girls against me for some time, I never hear from them again. I was only with them for three years but during that time, although I was in no way the perfect step-father, I did give them everything I could in terms of love, support and so on. It was invariably me who took them to the park, even on Sunday mornings when I might have been out the night before 'til the early hours.

Maybe it's in their best interests that all contact is severed. But it hurts.

2008

the time of my life

It is Christmas Day. I have a plan. For once I'm going to spend it alone, as a test of my ability to enjoy this special day without all the normal hullabaloo, and without feeling lonely because I'm single. I have bought a turkey and all the trimmings, several bottles of wine and port, and I'm going to enjoy cooking properly for once, and spoiling myself. But before all that, this morning I'm taking the chain ferry across the mouth of Poole Harbour to the Isle of Purbeck on the other side. I have never done this before and it feels like a trip into the unknown, not least because it has started to snow quite heavily and visibility is deteriorating.

I drive off the ferry and on for several miles, through the small village of Studland, and on out on a twisty road that rises and falls as it winds through what I can see of the beautiful countryside. After several more miles I start to climb again, and on my left I can just make out a snow-covered wood fringing a sloping field. At the top of the rise the wood comes down to meet the road as it curves to the right, and there's a small footpath sign. I park my car a little further on and walk back.

The wood is enchanting as I make my way up

through its snowy folds. The path bends round to the left and after only a short while I suddenly come across a sizeable stag, tall, proud and statuesque, standing stock still on the path about twenty feet ahead. I freeze too. I guess the poor visibility and our silent footsteps on the snow mean we've seen each other far later than normal. He is magnificent as he stares me out. In my peripheral vision I slowly become aware of the herd off to my right, at least twenty of them, watching us just as intently as we're watching each other. Time seems to stand still. But eventually, sensing I'm no real threat, he moves off into the undergrowth – slowly at first before picking up pace and jumping majestically through the undergrowth, showing just who is boss of the forest.

I feel exhilarated to be in nature so raw and real. It has been a long time. It fills my soul to be here in this enchanting place. I follow the path on up until I come out onto open pasture. I stumble over the uneven ground because the snow is thickening and visibility is worsening, until on the far side I'm dimly aware that I'm looking out across a valley and onto the next snow-covered ridge. I take a picture using the camera on my ageing phone, which isn't at all sophisticated.

It will later emerge that this picture is wonderfully atmospheric, and that I'm stood on top of the Purbeck Ridge at a place called Nine Barrow Down – with Swanage at the end of the valley to my left, and the infamous Corfe Castle at the end to my right. This is somewhere I will come back to again and again. It feels like home.

I left Southend in the summer. Not long before I'd dropped in on Bournemouth on the way back from working in the West Country and took a stroll along the endless expanse of sand. It was a beautiful sunny day and I thought, 'I could easily live here.' Indeed I started to do some limited visualisation of finding a gorgeous home to rent near the beach. So when I knew it was time to leave Liz and the girls behind I got on the internet and immediately saw exactly what I was looking for in Westbourne, two minutes from the sea. I arranged to see it the next morning.

It was a good job, because it turned out it had only just become available and I was the first person to view. A top-floor flat with huge living-room windows reaching right up into the eaves, it also had several skylights, making it one of the most light and airy homes I'd ever seen. The agent already had a long list of viewers eager to see it after me, so I did the only sensible thing I could and took it straight away. It was the only flat I looked at, and I never once regretted it.

I already had a fair bit of furniture from my last place in Southend. This included a gorgeous wooden bed, an incredibly robust and heavy dining room table and chairs, and a huge L-shaped sofa that Mike and I spent about three hours trying to get out of the door when he came up to help me move – my own fault for not watching more closely how the guys who delivered it manoeuvred it in the first place.

But that last flat had been relatively small, whereas now I had a large place that I could really go to town on. I chanced upon a shop not far away that imported lots of items from Thailand, which included several pairs of life-sized Thai-style Buddha heads selling at a very reasonable price. Although I'm no Buddhist I do have a lot of time for some aspects of their thinking, so I bought two pairs on the first visit. Then another pair on the next. Then another after that. I went just a little Buddha crazy.

Some months later I was in the shop again, ferreting around towards the back, when there he was, tucked right away... a large, seated, silver Buddha, about three feet high. I pulled him out. He was beautiful. There were quite a few women in the shop and as I took him to the till I heard every single one say, 'Oh my God, I love him, I have to have him!' And they didn't mean me. I know it wasn't very in keeping with what would most likely be his own views about nonattachment and materialism, but I held on tight. 'Bryan' has been with me ever since, through thick and thin. I don't see him as a possession, but he's the only supposedly inanimate thing in my life that I'd seriously rather not be without.

Rather less impressive was when I saw a huge framed photograph of a real Buddha in a shop near Southampton, and bought that too. I have two lifelong friends I've know since kindergarten aged four, Richard and Adrian, and I persuaded the latter to help me pick it up in his Volkswagen camper. We strapped it to the roof, but not very well, and if we exceeded 30 mph it started to lift up at the front. So it was a lengthy journey. Made even less rewarding when, on our eventual arrival at my flat, we found it was so big it wouldn't fit up the stairs without me cutting the picture out of the huge, expensive frame. Talk about nonattachment.

My time in my flat in Westbourne is a wonderful period in my life. I am predominantly single, not even having any dates of note for much of the time, but I'm truly contented. One of my favourite things is to walk into the centre of town along the beach on a Saturday evening, have a night out with a few drinks and a bit of dancing – I don't care if I'm alone or not – and then return down the promenade in the early hours with the beach all to myself, dancing to music on my headphones all the way. For me these are some of the most spiritual experiences of my entire life – and I mean that in the genuine sense.

I also love to return to the chain ferry so I can explore the Isle of Purbeck more. Every time it feels as if I'm taking a mini holiday, switching from the relative metropolis of Bournemouth and Poole into the wild unknowns of the Purbeck Ridge and beyond. I can see the ridge up ahead as I stand on the top deck, eager with anticipation about what I'll discover this time.

I visit my enchanted wood in better weather and encounter the deer every time – although never the stag again. I climb up onto the ridge and see the breathtaking view across the valley that was previously shrouded from me by the snow. I walk along it for several miles in each direction – to Old Harry's Rocks to the left, and to the picturesque village of Corfe, overlooked by its ruined castle, to the right.

I discover the quaint charm of Swanage, and further down the coast the more bustling seaside town of Weymouth, both of which I fall in love with. One day I venture further still on the beautiful coast road to Bridport, and stop in Abbotsbury, which is overlooked by the somewhat forlorn ruin of St Catherine's Chapel perched on top of the hill between the village and the sea. I enter a small gallery and am rather taken by a small driftwood mirror – until I see the exorbitant price. I think, 'I can do better than that myself, and for a fraction of the cost!'

In no time I'm scouring the south Dorset coast searching for driftwood. I learn that this must already be a serious pastime – even a job – for a lot of people, because much of the really good stuff is already long gone. Yet I also learn that I have a knack for using relatively ordinary pieces, especially cheap pine strips from broken-up pallets, that because of their grey patina can be turned into beautiful mirror surrounds. I set up a workshop in my living room, and the floor is often covered with shavings and sawdust. I don't care. Probably for the first time since I built my own race bikes I'm being creative with my hands, and I love every minute of it.

The trips to collect driftwood are events in themselves. Whole days out where I excitedly comb the various beaches along the Jurassic Coast – at Chapman's Pool, Kimmeridge, Worbarrow and Mupe Bays, Lulworth Cove and Durdle Door – then struggle back up cliff paths with bags and sometimes large planks arrayed around various parts of my body, while tourists look on as if I'm completely mad.

But the best hunting ground of all is the geological enigma that is Chesil Beach: a huge shingle bank that stretches west from Weymouth for about eighteen miles, cut off from the mainland for most of its length by a shallow lagoon. I learn that this is a real treasure trove for the driftwood hunter – but only if you're prepared to trek down it for at least a mile as the loose shingle retards your every step, sucking your energy despite the mounting excitement. Because once you do get beyond the range of where most people give up, then you're into relatively virgin territory.

The first time I get this far I can't believe my luck. In among the sad detritus of the modern world, with all its discarded plastics and so on, I discover so many truly unique and gorgeous pieces that I fill two bags and a rucksack, take them back to the car, then return and fill them all again. By the end I'm exhausted but elated. Several subsequent trips prove nearly as fruitful, until I've personally exhausted this source for at least a couple of years. With all this wonderful material to work with I branch out from mirrors, making lamps, barometers, clocks, shelves, notice boards and all sorts. In the end I make upwards of forty different pieces of driftwood art over several years.

In the summer of 2009 I also decide to celebrate my fiftieth year in style. I start with a highly debauched but terrifically fun week in Ibiza with an old friend, Neil, who still likes dance culture as much as I do – and who knows all the right people to get us on the VIP list at the top clubs. I rarely frequented clubs when I was younger, so I'm almost living my life backwards, but that feels fine to me.

I need a few days to recover when I get back but then, with minimal training, I crack on with the highly contrasting part two of my celebration – walking the South West Coast Path from Swanage to Weymouth. I carry a rucksack, small tent and sleeping bag on my back, and I know it will be beautiful but tough – the path undulates massively following the various cliff formations, so there are lots of steep climbs followed by equally challenging descents. Nor am I a real walker, I've only been getting into it in mild form since I arrived in Dorset, and I normally carry nothing at all. Although my driftwood collecting has conditioned me a bit, this will be a whole new level of challenge.

The first day, from Durlston Castle to a campsite just above Kimmeridge village, takes at least ten hours and nearly kills me – not least because the old path down to Chapman's Pool has just collapsed and I have to skirt inland, adding several miles to what was already the longest leg of my journey. I hardly have the energy to erect my tent in the twilight, and I collapse into my sleeping bag.

But when the next day dawns I feel fine, and make much shorter work of the second leg to arrive at a campsite above Durdle Door in good time. After a relaxing evening, the final leg the following day is even shorter, and I make it to a campsite just above Osmington Mills by early afternoon. I enjoy a long luxurious swim in their pool and feel it's a job well done – nothing to a seasoned walker, but not bad for a beginner like me. Better still, every time I visit a part of that coastline I can look far to the left and right and feel a sense of pride about how far I walked in those three days.

Nor is the driftwood artwork the end of my new-found creativity. Not long after my epic walk I see an advert for a classic 500cc, 4-cylinder Honda, a semi-race bike that has been used in hill climbs and not run for over ten years. I have always hankered after one of these, and it has the most gorgeous, one-off, race-style tank, painted in vivid red. That is enough for me. The rest of the bike is a bit of a heap but I don't care.

I am not in the mood to go racing again, but a café racer for the road will really fit the bill. The bike is in the north of England, and I don't even go to see it, I simply pay up and have it delivered. Nor do I have a garage to work on it, or a vice, or any of the workshop equipment you really need to rebuild a bike like this. I just have the pavement outside my flat, a reasonable toolkit, some ingenuity – and some pretty accommodating neighbours.

It takes me right through to the following summer to finish it. At one point I have an entire replacement wiring loom spread out across my living room floor, and it's a real logical challenge to incorporate all the non-standard lights, indicators and other parts that need to be fitted to make it road legal. As far as the engine is concerned, all I do is change the oil and filter, check the ignition timing and valve clearances, and clean out the carburettors. Considering it hasn't run for over a decade I'm overjoyed when after only a few coughs and splutters it bursts into life. The road-legal exhaust silencer I've fitted still allows it to make a gorgeous roar when the throttle is opened up, even though it's really not very fast compared to a modern machine. With a matching bright red mudguard and seat, the completed bike looks fantastic too.

On my few local test rides to get it ready for its MOT I find it's quite hard to ride, with a very cramped riding position for my 6' 2" frame, despite rear-set footrests. But I get used to it over time. The whole road registration process is a bit of a nightmare because I don't know anything about the bike's history, but we get there in the end. Indeed just in time for a serious road trip – to the Isle of Man.

While in Bournemouth I've been doing a few talks about my books, one at the local Positive Living Group, which has a network across the south. When I get there the organiser asks if I'd like to lead a guided meditation to get the ball rolling. I am not sure that I could even if I wanted to, but luckily a lean, shaven-headed chap standing nearby kindly offers to do it for me. With his extensive moustache and goatee beard he looks a little like Fu Manchu, but he has a kind smile. What is more, despite us never having met and him knowing little about my work, he proceeds to tell the group they should keep an open mind even though they may find some of what I have to say a little challenging.

How right he is! During the Q & A session at the end one woman walks out because I dare to question one aspect of the work of her chosen guru, the great Eckhart Tolle, whose *Power of Now* has had such a positive impact on millions of people. She slams the door as she leaves the church hall, but I get the impression she might have form for this kind of behaviour.

In any case Ken, or Kenny as I affectionately call him, soon becomes one of my closest friends, along with his partner Pam. What is more he used to have a motorbike himself many years ago, so I persuade him to buy a classic Honda too and we plan a trip to the Isle of Man at very short notice. With both bikes almost completely untested and laden with luggage, we head for Liverpool. Well, actually we first head for Blandford, where Kenny goes straight on instead of taking the ring road and I'm already contemplating making the trip alone while I wait for him to realise his mistake. But finally we're reunited.

It soon becomes clear that we both have to stop around every fifty miles to stretch our legs. Neither of us has ridden regularly for years and we're out of practice – plus my bike is so cramped for room I look like a spider draped over it, all arms and legs. That aside we make good progress until we're nearing the end. For some time Kenny has been racing along at over ninety, head down over the handlebars, yellow anorak flapping in the wind and elbows raised – I can just sense the look of crazed determination that must be under his helmet, accompanied by the faintest of manic grins. But now I see that his back wheel is starting to meander from side to side, and on closer inspection the tyre is getting flatter and flatter. He has a puncture.

Kenny of course remains totally oblivious to such niceties, even when the weaving starts to get worse. I am trying to nurse my engine given that it's not been run for over a decade, but I realise I will have to give it more revs to get past him and wave him in to the hard shoulder, which I do. We miss the ferry and have to stay in a B & B while we wait for a repair shop to open the next day. But we have a nice curry, and the added bonus of the lady on reception kindly informing me I look like a Transformer in my new one-piece leathers and white boots – my trademark when I was racing.

When we finally get across to the Island we are

staying with my old mate Chris, who is still racing and even winning despite advancing years. We have a whale of a time, a proper boy's holiday, and it's one of my fondest memories. What is more now our bodies are acclimatised we only stop twice the whole way home – and, apart from Kenny's puncture and a broken plug cap for me, the bikes behave perfectly throughout.

If I was to be stereotypical I'd suggest this will be the last time Pam lets him off the leash before she gets him properly under control. So I won't be as unkind as to say that because I love them both dearly, almost as surrogate parents or older siblings, while they never tire of telling me that they see me as a wayward child. All I *can* report is that for one reason or another we've never enjoyed a repeat performance.

I still have plenty of training work coming in, so I've now paid off all debts accumulated during the hard times and financially I'm comfortable at last. Moreover driftwood and bikes aside I still have time for writing and research, and in fact before I left Southend I started on a new edition of my original book under the amended title *The Big Book of the Soul* – to distinguish it from the little one. This is a pretty serious rewrite, with lots of new evidential cases and detailed analysis, and it takes some time to complete.

On top of this during a conference in the summer of 2009 I meet Hazel, who is now Andy Tomlinson's right-hand woman in his regression academy, and after much initial reluctance on my part she persuades me that I should actually train as a therapist myself. So later that year I commence with basic hypnosis, then on into full regression training the following year.

This turns out to be a cracking idea. Not only does it give me hope of an alternative career where I might actually be able to help people one-on-one with their problems, but I also get to meet like-minded people and strike up a number of important new friendships. Apart from when I was with Liz, ever since I started my spiritual research I've not really been able to talk about it to friends or family. I can mention it in passing, and sometimes they're interested for a while but, if I go too far, eyes soon glaze over. So it's incredibly refreshing to at last be able to talk openly and at length about topics that really interest me. It is as if I'm no longer split into two people, and am becoming whole again.

The regression training at Gaunts House north of Wimborne takes the form of four 4-day modules spread over about a year, with more or less the same group of around fifteen people. It brings us incredibly close together when we're practising our therapy skills on each other, because as you might imagine a great deal of personal baggage or 'stuff' comes out. Indeed an essential part of the training is that we sort out our own stuff before trying to work with clients.

Once I do start practising as a therapist on the whole I find it immensely rewarding, and I certainly have some successes where I'm genuinely able to help people get past their emotional blockages and so on. But after a year or so I find the clients coming to me are becoming more and more challenging, and I'm not always able to deal with them myself. One in particular starts choking so badly, with me unable to bring her out of the experience, that I'm worried she might die on the couch in front of me. Eventually only Andy himself is able to sort out her problem, but that incident is pretty much enough for me. In any case, while I'm certainly not a *bad* therapist, I have close colleagues and friends who are much better suited to the work. So I decide that it's more important for me to concentrate on what I *am* most suited for, which is writing and research.

Talking of which, during my training I'm regressed into a number of past lives, most very different from each other. But one in particular stands out, because of it's similarity to that first regression with Andy recounted in the last chapter. I don't have a transcript of the session, but from my notes the life commences with me as a fairly junior member of a monastic order making a copy of a Latin Bible – apparently I'm very good at the fancy gilding of some of the letters. I then report that I've left the order because they've forgotten the true message of Christ, which is all about unconditional love. So I'm travelling around preaching, and brave people take me in wherever I go, although obviously many are afraid. I am arrested regularly but the authorities always seem to let me go – I report that it may be they're afraid of riots of some sort.

Finally I'm arrested and this time I know they're not going to let me out. I've become too dangerous and they can't let me carry on. But nor are they going to risk a public death and martyrdom. Instead they're just going to let me rot. I experience being led to a cell, and even at the prospect of long-term isolation I'm holding my dignity together.

But from the doorway I see a large wooden chair with shackles for the arms and feet, and on a table next to it a metal helmet, designed to cover the entire head with only a slit for food and water. I'm gripped with terror and keep screaming, 'No! Not that! Please kill me instead! Anything but that!' I relive being shackled to the chair, and in trance I'm breathing very heavily as they fit the helmet on my head. I report that, from that moment on, every time I nod off to sleep its weight jerks me awake again. Even so it seems to be many years before my body finally gives up. Nothing about this experience is pleasant.

Another fantasised ego-trip in which I'm the hero tortured for telling the truth? Quite possibly. But this time there's an interesting postscript. The following week I happened to mention the experience in an email to an acquaintance from a spiritual group – and the following morning she received an unsolicited email from another member of the group: 'The night before last I had a really weird dream. I can't remember all of it apart from there being a man's head that was being kept imprisoned, but he was fully alive.'

Although I've deliberately never used any personal experiences containing possible evidence for past lives in my research books, another interesting event does occur at around this time. On a glorious Sunday afternoon in midwinter I find myself taking a walk from the Hardy Monument in the countryside south-west of Dorchester to the village of Portesham nearer the coast. After meandering down through a valley and up the other side, I come to a ridge that overlooks the village.

As I'm traversing the beautiful grassy descent I suddenly feel that I want to be 'given' a feeling of a past life. Perhaps this isn't surprising inasmuch as I've been newly researching *spontaneous* past-life memories in adults for *The Big Book of the Soul*. But having said that I've never before felt such a sudden and strong desire to experience something tangible while in my normal, conscious state.

I immediately get the sense of a big, powerful man wearing a heavy greatcoat and big, heavy boots. I can feel he's tired, hungry and poor. I walk on for a few steps, just trying to get a sense of who this man is, and suddenly the name 'William Darrow' flashes into my head, followed by the year '1812'. I intuit that this is when he was born, and even before I can articulate a question about his year of death in my head I get '1865'. Immediately afterwards I also get the name 'Ann', which I presume could have been his wife.

I have no pen, paper or other means of making a record so, because my conventional memory is not what it was, I know if I try to get much more new information it will push out what I already have. So I don't try. Of course I also know how the mind can play tricks, meaning I'm not at all confident that even what I have will actually signify anything. Nevertheless, because it seems to me that it's the view down over the village that has prompted my 'vision', I assume that I might have sensed someone who was connected with Portesham itself. So I make my way to the church to see if I can find anything.

There are precious few headstones in the

graveyard, nor can I find the name Darrow on any of the graves or notices inside the church, and there's no one about to ask for further details. When I get home I search the internet for someone of that name connected to the village, but again draw a complete blank. So I decide that, even if it's not just my imagination playing tricks, I'm not going to be able to verify the names and dates I've come up with.

Then the following morning I wake up early, remembering that of course these days census and other historical data is available online. So I visit one of the many websites and straight away I see that both the 1851 and 1861 census show only one entry for a William Darrow, meaning – perhaps surprisingly – this isn't a common name at all. A good start. But when I click on the entry for the 1851 version it turns out he was apparently born in Norfolk about 1820. Not so good. Without much hope I then click on the entry for the 1861 version, expecting to find the same person. But this William Darrow appears to be totally different. He lived in Warwickshire – ok, people move about – but what really makes my spine tingle is when I read he was born in Lancashire... in *approximately 1811*!

How much of a coincidence can it be that I picked a name for whom there are so few entries, and then got the date right within one year – and possibly bang on, given the record indicates it's an approximation only? Admittedly this person seems to have had nothing to do with Portesham, but that's only an assumption I made at the time. It is well known that a particular view or situation can trigger a past-life memory, but it doesn't have to be the exact same thing, just something similar. Trekking across country, cold and tired, looking forward to some sort of shelter as he saw his destination come into view – all this might well have been a familiar story for the man I now dub 'Big Bill'.

Nor is that all. I see that the criminal registers for 1791-1892 show two entries for that name, with trials that took place a few years either side of the 1861 census, in 1855 and 1862 – and in the same county, Warwickshire. *If* – and I accept it's still a very big if – but *if* this is a former incarnation of mine, what had I been up to, and what was my punishment?

The first trial saw George and William Darrow acquitted of 'horse stealing' at the quarterly sessions in Coventry. Was George my brother?

At the second the pair were less fortunate. Convicted of 'assault with intent to rob' at the quarterly sessions in Birmingham, they were each sentenced to six months in jail. These criminal records for what must surely be the same person, living in the right county in the right period, suggest he may well have been poor and forced to steal to make ends meet. Not so surprising for the period, perhaps – but the person I sensed was certainly big enough to have committed assault without much fear.

By now fully engaged in the hunt for this echo from the past I search the death records, but they show only one entry for that name, in Warrington in 1843, which cannot be the same person. Yet we have to remember these records are not infallible or complete, so this is disappointing but in no way weakens the case.

Now all I have left is to turn my attention to Big Bill's possible wife. The marriage records for 1837-2005 show only two entries for this *entire* period for William Darrow – who would believe this would be *such* an uncommon name? One is dated 1860 in Dudley, the other 1873 in Liverpool. Clearly the second entry would be too late if the date of death I received was correct, but the first entry could well relate to the same person given the closeness of the location. So I click on it with some trepidation, but little genuine hope that I'll score another direct hit. I then find that because of the way these records work they show two possible spouses. But one of them is... *Ann* Shedden Dunn.

I am more than happy to hear from any statisticians about the likelihood of all this just being random chance – I left all that behind at university long ago. But it seems to me this result isn't entirely without interest. Remember too that, unlike the other past lives I've mentioned that had a possibly ego-driven, heroic aspect, Big Bill led an unremarkable life of which I could have absolutely no knowledge in the normal course of events.

On the writing front, towards the end of 2009 I put together another simple little pocket book called *Your Holographic Soul (and how to make it work for you)*. This uses a question and answer format, and the manuscript receives input from a team of five or six close colleagues and friends.

Almost immediately that's finished we're at

Gaunts again for one of my therapy training courses when we decide to experiment with some channelling after dinner. The way this works is that several volunteers take themselves into a meditative state, and then open themselves up to act as channels for entities from other planes of consciousness to speak through them. A good friend and one of Andy's most gifted trainers, Janet, starts to shake violently during this session – which initially seems rather worrying because we all know she's not prone to exaggeration or ego.

Then when she starts talking she reports that her consciousness has temporarily been taken over by a representative of a group calling themselves 'the council'. What is more some of the answers to our initial questions are so unexpected and non-intuitive, yet interesting, that we conclude these are definitely nonhuman entities with a different perspective. (For anyone interested in trying something similar, please note that not only does Janet 'take herself off to sit under her favourite tree' while the entities using her do their work, but she has also learned to put a great many safety measures in place when she does this kind of work, to ensure nothing untoward can happen.)

As a group we decide this is too good an opportunity to miss, and that we should make use of the wisdom of these entities to find out more, especially given that many people are becoming very excited in the run up to 2012. This is reported as the end of an era in the Mayan calendar that will either bring about major catastrophes or mark the high point of the 'shift in human consciousness' that people have been talking about for some time – possibly even both.

As I did with *The Wisdom of the Soul* I put together a list of questions we want to ask, then we convene at Hazel's flat in Bristol for another session with Janet and the council. To summarise their most important messages, they suggest there will be a series of natural catastrophes over several years that will significantly reduce the human population on Earth – from a higher perspective perhaps no bad thing given the extent to which we're overexploiting its resources – and that the 'shift' is an incredible opportunity that's been known about, planned for and eagerly awaited in other dimensions for thousands of years.

I make transcripts of the recordings, edit them to make logical sense, and pass them to the others for input and revisions. We self-publish the result in the pocket-sized *Future of the Soul*, and with several of us involved we sell most of the 2000-copy print run in fairly short order.

The trouble is a great deal of what the council predicts doesn't come to pass, and not just because the timings are out. I am not suggesting for one moment that everyone involved in whatever dimension wasn't operating with complete integrity, but in hindsight this kind of exercise is clearly fraught with difficulty. The general idea of the shift may still be correct, but other than that making predictions about details seems to be something to be avoided.

In a way that's a comforting thought. Perhaps this exercise really does show that the future is uncertain precisely because, as creator gods, we're manifesting this reality both individually and collectively as we go along. Which idea is, of course, entirely tied in with the law of attraction – and so central to this narrative that you won't have to be patient for much longer before I treat it to the full analysis and discussion it deserves.

2011

my dark night of the soul

I am staring at my reflection in the small mirror above the sink of the converted Mercedes van I call home. I have dubbed it 'the Love Bus' in better times, but now it is devoid of that essential quality and has been for some time. I am startled to see bruises on my forehead. Stark, yellow and purple reminders of the inner turmoil of the night before... of me pummelling myself in despair and frustration at my plight.

My life has been spiralling out of control for a while. Everything seems to be conspiring against me. But one thing has kept me going throughout this most painful period. My love for a woman, and her love for me. She's married with children, it's complicated, and not without its own pain. We plan a future together, but only after a long and painful process do she and her husband separate, and even after that they're forced back together by love of their children – anything to take away their pain. I still love her but she can offer me no hope.

Yet I cling to that love. It's all I have.

Then suddenly, the final bombshell. So totally unexpected, to me at least, that I've never even remotely contemplated it. Although back with her husband she's now fallen massively for *someone else*. Love at first sight. The real deal. Her bond with him is even stronger than the one she shared with me, and she simply cannot resist.

There's no deliberate intent to hurt me, but in an instant I'm an afterthought, a mere footnote to the new things in her life. I have no idea if she'll be able to achieve the lifelong happiness with him that she never could with me. But it doesn't matter anyway, because I don't matter any more.

I was already right on the precipice, and now I feel it crumbling under my feet. I am in an agony of doubt and rejection and above all fear about what is happening to me. Always the fear.

So what the hell do I do?

Towards the end of 2009 the training work I was being given by Parity started to slow down, but to me it was still a surprise when the following spring they went bust. They had been acquired by another company about a year before and evidently the merger didn't work. The problem was they were one of the biggest providers of

PRINCE2 training in the country, so their demise flooded the market with trainers. Moreover with me being a relative newcomer to the scene with few contacts, I was last on the list to find alternative work. On top of that, the economy was taking a real downturn as the effects of the infamous 'credit crunch' started to bite. Over the next couple of years I'd be offered a mere handful of courses by other, smaller companies.

So already by the middle of the year I was in serious trouble financially and couldn't afford to remain in my lovely flat by the sea. What little savings I had were already gone, but Andy Tomlinson graciously offered to let me share his flat in Christchurch rent free. He was an absolute saviour to me at this point in my life, and for that, and for introducing me to project management training in the first place, I will be eternally grateful.

During this time I was still seeing a small number of regression clients, but my main hope of generating income again became my books and research. I took the opportunity to rewrite *Genesis Unveiled* under the revised title *The History of the Soul* and, just as with the *Big Book of the Soul*, I took out elements I felt were no longer that strong and added new ones in their place. Of course this rewrite was partly intended to run alongside *The Future of the Soul* that we'd published not long before. I also spent hundreds of hours preparing Kindle versions of all my books. All this came on top of some time back having managed to persuade Waterstones to stock them in the UK, similarly Barnes and Noble in the US. But sadly none of this had any significant impact on sales.

Of course I'd been giving talks about my work ever since I started, particularly spreading the word about Rational Spirituality. Some had been to quite large audiences, others less so – oh yes, I went through the humbling experience of turning up at a church hall in the middle of nowhere on a rainy Tuesday night to talk to about five people, including the organiser. I earned my spurs. But I felt now must be the time to ramp things up again.

My first plan was to get away from it all for a bit, in a way I never had before. Kenny kindly accepted my offer that he might lend me the money for a plane ticket to Thailand, flying out just after New Year 2011. My destination was the well-known 'Sanctuary', on the island of Koh

Phangan, where I intended to run a series of workshops over maybe two or three months. I had tried to organise this in advance, but in the end it became clear I was just going to have to get out there and wing it.

Unfortunately it didn't work out at all as I'd planned. For a start I arranged to stay on the next beach down, not at the Sanctuary itself, to save money. But some of the people on my beach had been there for some time and weren't very spiritual at all – I just didn't like the atmosphere. Nor was I massively impressed by the residents at the Sanctuary. It may well have been me being overly judgmental, but listening into conversations in the main bar-cum-café I couldn't help but detect what I felt was a not inconsiderable level of spiritual ego, while to describe it as cliquey is an understatement. That is how I found it anyway, I'm sure others would disagree.

Worse than all of that, though, every time I trekked through the jungle to visit the office to try to sort out my workshops the organiser I'd been in email contact with wasn't there. Nor did she ever leave any message in response to my messages as to when she would be available to talk to me. Maybe I didn't try to see her as hard as I should have done, but my inner voices were increasingly telling me this wasn't working and I should get out while I still had the money to do so. So after only two weeks I phoned Andy and he kindly said I could move back into his flat any time I liked.

On a positive note I learned that I'm useless at travelling far afield on my own, and it's always good to know one's own weaknesses. I also got to live in a beach hut on stilts for two weeks, which I would recommend to anyone, even if I did feel rather lonely and exposed most of that time – especially when the local monkeys delighted in pelting the corrugated roof with nutshells at night when I was trying to sleep.

Best of all I got to attend a secret rave party in the jungle – and dancing all night with a band of spaced-out hippies, all crowing like cocks as the sun came up through the trees, still ranks as one of my all-time favourite experiences. This despite that fact I'd forgotten to bring any deodorant, forcing one young lady to drag the less-than-fragrant tee-shirt from my back – leaving my fat, white, winter body basking in all its glory on the dance floor.

More bad news followed when I got back. I had been given the lifeline of a week's training course by one of the companies I occasionally worked for, and was staying up in the Midlands, when I got a call telling me my brother John had been taken into hospital with prostate cancer – but that he should survive at least 'til I returned. He had always been a bit of a loner from a family perspective. He knew he was gay from a very early age, but back in the 1950s and early 1960s it had to be kept under wraps. Plus Syd was from a generation and background that was never going to easily accept such a perceived weakness in his eldest son – at least not until he was into his seventies, when he softened somewhat, but by that time John had already suffered for years.

I was quite close to him because he felt he could confide in me. He was even proud to take me to gay clubs sometimes, knowing that I could look after myself. But he kept his illness quiet until the last minute, and went downhill much faster than expected – which was obviously a blessing for him, but it meant he passed before the end of the week and I didn't even get to see him.

One silver lining of my Thailand trip was that

when I got back I made plans to run a series of similar seminars-cum-workshops at Gaunts and at the College of Psychic Studies in London, where I'd previously given a number of successful talks. There would be a total of 24 running from April to December. I spent what little money I had having posters and fliers printed, and advertising the events on various websites. When the first few received minimal interest and had to be cancelled I was disappointed but not defeated. But as time went on, each cancellation became like a knife in my stomach. In the end not a single event ran.

Also around this time I started the relationship with Katherine introduced in the opening passage. A trainee therapist in the year behind mine at Andy's academy, we'd been becoming closer for some months, albeit that I knew she was married. But when she disclosed just how unhappily things developed – although to be fair to myself, after my experience with Liz and John, I did try to keep it reasonably platonic for as long as I could. Then in no time at all she quite unexpectedly lost her father, with whom she'd had a somewhat strained relationship, and I had to become her rock. She was phoning me sometimes four or five times a day, but I loved her so I was happy to be there for her. She says I taught her how to live again – that there was light at the end of the tunnel after all.

But any affair of this nature is difficult, and I'm not sure anyone really likes sneaking around behind others' backs. Although their marriage was to all intents and purposes dead and had been for some years, even after she finally told her husband she wanted to separate, for many months he refused to even contemplate it.

Now, before I'm accused of being a heartless encourager of adultery, I accept that as a man who has never been married or had children of my own I'm not best placed to enter the debate about whether or not it's best that children remain in a loveless but stable environment. He was clearly a good father, but I got the impression that more than anything he was something of a control freak towards Katherine and he just didn't want to give up that control. Not only that, I had strong intuitions he was seeing someone himself – not that this stopped him making all sorts of threats to Katherine about me. I was later proved right.

In any case, coupled with her living near Bristol, all this made it hard to see each other except for occasional snatched trysts. So I was desperately short of money, with virtually no therapy or training work, my books weren't selling despite my best efforts, my series of seminars was turning out to be a cruel joke, I was living on the kindness of others, and I was frustrated at hardly ever being able to see the woman I loved. At this point I received what felt at the time like several more massive kicks in the teeth.

Early in the year I'd met the UK agent of the well-known US author and past-life therapist Dolores Cannon. This person had heard me speaking and apparently been impressed, so we provisionally arranged to run a seminar in London later in the year with Dolores and I as the speakers, concentrating on what changes 2012 might hold in store. Dolores herself agreed because she was familiar with my work, in which I referenced her own books. But all the proposals for content and so on came from me.

Within a few months of this meeting it was fairly common knowledge amongst my friends and acquaintances that I was struggling with my own seminars and other things. But I was absolutely gobsmacked when I received a call from Dolores' agent telling me she – the agent, not Dolores – didn't want me to be involved in my own seminar any more! Nor could I obtain any explanation from her, apart from, 'I don't think your head is in the right place,' before she put the phone down on me. I couldn't believe it. I have been used to working in the professional world, and whatever personal problems one may be suffering the show goes on with full commitment. The best way I can describe the phone call was that it felt like I was being dumped from a relationship with no proper explanation. Totally bizarre, and totally unprofessional.

So imagine just how cruelly shocked I then was when I found out from Katherine that Andy's deputy Hazel, with whom she was by now best buddies, had arranged to take my place at the Cannon seminar. It didn't take a genius to work out where her agent had got her information. Nor was I overly happy that Katherine seemed to think this was all perfectly fine behaviour. Some spiritual people tend to adopt the attitude that they can pretty much behave how they like because it's always up to each of us how we respond to any given situation – and if we get 'triggered' that's our problem. While this may sometimes be true, it can also be an excuse for seriously shabby behaviour.

Nothing daunted I arranged to run another seminar later in the year, this time with my good friend Sue Stone, the Bournemouth-based life coach and author who I'd met when she ran the local Positive Living Group. It would be grandly titled 'Personal Empowerment for 2012 and Beyond', and alongside us would be Andy and the physicist and spiritual author Dr Jude Currivan – with whom I'd corresponded and swapped books for some time.

Now Sue had always been pretty good at organising events and at motivating people, but as this one drew closer I could sense a distinct lack of enthusiasm. We had agreed she would undertake the bulk of the marketing and ticket sales for a larger share of the return, but these had been poor. Then with only about a month to go she dropped the bombshell that she didn't want to be involved any more. I understood that she had just arranged to make an appearance on a television programme and wanted to concentrate on that, but I guess – especially when this came on top of everything else – in my own head I couldn't help but feel let down. She offered to let me take it all over, but at such a late stage I felt the only sensible thing to do was ask her to cancel it.

In the meantime back in the summer I've had to move out of Andy's, partly because his girlfriend is coming to live with him, but in any case I shouldn't outstay my welcome. Kenny comes to my rescue again, lending me the money to buy an old Mercedes 709D race van. I have a month to convert the Love Bus into a proper mobile home before moving out, and I work incredibly hard. But in the end I am, I hope justifiably, proud of my efforts.

It takes a week to remove all the aluminium panelling and partitioning, then I insulate the walls and ceiling before covering it all in pine tongue-and-groove cladding. I build a strong base for a raised double bed at the back, incorporating a sliding door to access the storage space underneath, and removable panels at the rear so that when the back door is open I can lie there and look at the stars. I install a completely new leisure battery, control panels and wiring system – even though my knowledge of electrics is minimal I manage to work it out by logic and trial and error. I cap it all off with a lovely log burner converted from a large gas bottle, with a flu running out through the roof. It already has a sink with running water and a two-ring gas hob, but no proper bathing or toilet facilities. A combined microwave, grill and oven completes the ensemble.

Of course I have to sell almost all of my lovely furniture at auction, for a pittance, so pretty much all I put into storage is my books, Buddhas and driftwood pieces. In fact because I've already moved around a lot in my life I've already got rid of a lot of the rubbish that most of us tend to accumulate, but now the process is really in earnest. Having said that it's actually incredibly liberating to get rid of almost all the inessentials pretty much for the first time since I went bankrupt. It is amazing how much stuff we cart around with us that we really don't need at all. I feel lighter, like I have nothing hanging around my neck and can just get up and go whenever I want.

What actually happens is I don't move around at

all, because Kenny and Pam are incredibly kind and let me park the Love Bus on the drive of their house in the village of Hazelbury Bryan in North Dorset, into which they've not long moved themselves. Once my few remaining possessions are installed in the bus it's cosy – ok, some would say pretty confined – yet certainly homely. It doesn't take long to get used to living in it, and as long as I'm hooked up to the mains and have access to a shower, toilet and washing machine there's really nothing I'm missing. Indeed there's no doubt that 'glamping' can be fun.

What is more, for all that this is probably the worst year of my life we still go out to country pubs, sometimes accompanied by our good friend Amanda from nearby Sherborne, and have some wonderful evenings full of love and laughter. They are all very close friends and, particularly with Kenny and Pam being highly qualified therapists themselves – him a hypnotherapist, her a counsellor – they're incredibly kind and understanding.

Of course seeing therapy clients is definitely no longer an option for me now I'm living in a bus, even if I wanted to – which by now I really don't.

There is still very little training work coming in, although each course I get is an absolute godsend financially. I even take all my driftwood pieces to a huge local fair that focuses on wood and wooden objects, but it's a complete disaster and I fail to sell a singe piece. Of course the prices may be slightly too high, but if they are then there's no way I can make a living from it.

So late in 2011, still desperately searching for a way to carry the message of Rational Spirituality to a wider audience, and to try to make some money to live on, I make my first attempt at writing fiction in the form of a relatively short novel called *The Man Who Didn't Die*. It tells the story of a man who has no interest in the spiritual side of life until he kills his wife in a car crash and leaves himself in a wheelchair. It also, unsurprisingly, tells the story of what happens to him *after* his death. It has some interesting plot twists, the characterisation isn't completely awful, and I'm delighted when I hear from Stephen – who we encountered in the opening chapter, and who I first met when we were both living in Southend – that Margaret really thinks I've found my niche.

Encouraged I quickly produce a sequel, *The Girl*

Who Learned to Live, which arguably is a better and more well-rounded piece of fiction. This time the heroine is held back by past-life issues that keep surfacing but only become clear towards the end, and again there are some nice little plot twists. Once more everyone who reads it loves it.

But neither book sells anything other than a handful of copies. However word of mouth operates, my books aren't triggering people to use it. So all the time I'm sinking further and further down. When I reflect I feel I've carried on battling against the odds, doing something I really believe in that's not just for me but should have a benefit to humanity or society as a whole – yet for what? I have now self-published more than ten books covering a wide range of spiritual topics in every conceivable way – complex research-based books, simple pocket ones, novels. Yet overall sales have steadily decreased, and recently they've dwindled to almost nothing. I am selling way, way less than when I only had one book to offer.

What is worse people hardly even talk to each other about my work any more, let alone to me. In the past people regularly wrote to tell me how much my books had helped them, sometimes even that I was a brilliant researcher. But not any more.

By this time I'm properly aware of the law of attraction – it would be hard not to be, what with the plethora of best-sellers and films that deal with the topic over the last decade. So I've been meditating every day for years, visualising every positive outcome conceivable, chanting manifestation mantras and developing 'vision boards' containing photos and text evocative of the life I want to lead. I know that my subconscious thoughts and beliefs can get in the way of me consciously manifesting the outcomes I desire, but during my therapy training I supposedly cleared my emotional blockages. What is more, even since then I've had close colleagues – the best therapists around – checking me for any that remain. All to no avail.

I have thought about ending it all plenty of times recently, lying alone on my bed in my cramped living space. Never worse than the night when I find myself beating my forehead with my fists in total despair and frustration. Frustration because I've had an expensive education, I'm reasonably intelligent and fit, I have all the advantages and I'm capable of so much – yet for some time now everything I've touched seems to have turned to dust.

What nobody works out or at least tells me, and what I don't recognise for myself at the time, is that I'm completely and utterly in 'victim mode' – and this holds true even though I've been trying so hard to get myself out of the situation. Moreover as long as I stay in that mode my plight will continue.

I get through all this somehow, not least supported by Katherine's love. But as I intimated in the opening passage even that's something of a double-edged sword, because it's giving me about as much pain as comfort. Even when her husband does finally agree to move out of the family home and it seems we might finally be able to make some time for each other, her two teenage boys react incredibly badly. One is even threatening suicide. Of course she can't be expected to handle this, so after an agonising further few months he moves back in. Our relationship is now effectively over, but it's still extremely hard to let go – for me at least, because her love feels like all I have left.

Then she hits me with the bombshell that I wouldn't have expected in a million years. She has met someone else, fallen madly in love, and in no time is arranging to live with him. Equally shattering after all we went through is that this time all goes smoothly and her children and husband quickly accept the situation – so it's pretty clear that her path must lie with him and not me. But it's still an incredibly painful blow, and feels like yet another rejection on a huge scale just when I need it least. I have been making a little progress in some other areas of my life, but this puts me right back on the tightrope.

So what *do* I do to cope?

The answer is... *love*.

Most of us have been in that place where the pain of just imagining two people together can make your heart literally break – where you feel a deep, physical pain in your chest. Just as that is happening to me on the first night after she breaks the news, a strong voice in my head says that one word, *love*, really clearly. This inner guidance seems to want me to keep pushing myself to face my fear by imagining them together. In fact I'm literally sweating as I force myself through a series of visualisations that end in my worst nightmare – the two of them being totally and lovingly intimate with each other.

Yet at that point, just as everything should be at its worst, I feel an intense burst of love shooting out from my chest towards the coupling pair – who will of course be blissfully unaware of any of this. It is hard to explain what's going on, but it's as if intense jealousy is replaced by happiness for what they've found – that their happiness is *my* happiness. I feel a tremendous release, and the pain vanishes instantly.

From that point on, any time I think of the two of them together I literally *smother* myself in a blanket of love, and the pain in my chest vanishes immediately – and stays vanished. It works every single time, without fail, over those first few weeks and even months. That is how I learn the truth of the saying, 'pain is inevitable but suffering is optional'. I am literally transmuting fear and pain into love.

Do I do anything else to cope? Of course – I write a book about it! *The Gift* is completed in about six weeks. I use my experiences of the last year or two to postulate the 'six aspects model' of deriving comfort and happiness from 1) our work and finances, 2) our hobby (if not the same), 3) our health, 4) our partner and children (if we have them), 5) our family and 6) our friends. I suggest that loss in one or two areas is reasonably easy to handle, but if you get to the point where you've only got one or two remaining as a positive in your life – in my case it was my physical health and just a few friends and family – it can be a real struggle to feel any sense of inner peace or self worth.

Of course I'm aware that a true Buddhist master of 'nonattachment' needs nothing external to give them peace. But cultivating that degree of self mastery isn't something that all human beings aspire to – irrespective of whether or not we're all capable of it, which isn't a judgement I'm prepared to make.

I also take this opportunity to talk about what I call 'the three timeless treasures of transformation': that is, *inner peace*, *conscious creation*, and *being love*. The first is what I've just been discussing. The third is the gift I discovered, on which the book's title is based. Meanwhile the second is intimately bound up with the law of attraction, which as we've seen repeatedly is a key aspect of our current narrative. So at this point in my life I'm definitely emphasising its importance. The problem is I still haven't developed the right broader context to put it into, in terms of a spiritual model where it can truly take centre stage. Rational Spirituality isn't it – but I haven't worked that out yet.

Most crucially of all, this gap in my understanding is what allows me to continue to behave like a victim.

2012

everything must change

It is later summer and I'm in an Indian cafe in Wembley, North London. Sitting across from me is my friend Todd Acamesis. An American by birth, for many years he's been practising taking his consciousness 'out-of-body' – or OOB for short – and has established himself as a leading pioneer in this area of research in the UK. It is no surprise to him that I have a long list of questions, and we start ploughing through them over dinner. The conversation is absorbing but intense, and now I've arrived at probably the most crucial question of all – at least for me at this point.

During a previous meeting some time ago Todd has told me how he's been meeting with an incredibly wise entity called Acamesis in the highest planes he's able to access, and after several visits has been shocked to realise it's just another aspect of *himself* – or of what he calls his own oversoul. This is why he has changed his surname. But I've had plenty of time to mull over this in the interim, and now I need more: 'Just how do you *know* he's part of you. How can you be so *sure*?'

His answer is swift and unequivocal: 'Ian, you just *know*. In OOB exploration everything is about sensing different vibratory patterns, different frequencies of energy. The first few times I met Acamesis I was blown away, he felt like the highest, wisest form of intelligence I could ever meet... an angel or even a god in his own right. But then on one journey, when I'd calmed down a bit and become more accustomed to his energy, it just hit me that the vibrational pattern he was exuding had a special quality because it exactly matched my own. For all I know he was shielding me 'til I was ready for the truth.'

Somehow I just *know* that's what he's going to say. In fact deep down I've known he was right in his identification ever since he first mentioned the idea. I just haven't wanted to accept that everything I thought I knew – that comforting, simple framework of Rational Spirituality I've spent more than a decade developing – has only been scratching the surface.

But now it's all out in the open, fully in my conscious awareness. Now all fear falls away. Of course it doesn't mean everything I've written before is necessarily *wrong* per se, it has just represented a certain level of understanding. But now it's time to push on again into what is, for me at least, uncharted territory. The *third* shock to my spiritual system has fully taken hold.

For many years before this I'd felt there was very little that could alter the Rational Spiritual worldview I'd developed as a result of the second shock to my spiritual system, which was discovering Michael Newton's interlife research. There might have been occasional tinkering at the edges, but nothing that forced me to make *significant* changes. It was rare even for me to become excited by any spiritual books or talks.

Then early in 2011 I attended a party in South London along with several acquaintances from the therapy world. The hostess was an inspirational speaker and author and had only recently met this tall American guy. She and her friends already had them practically married to each other, and I could tell it was making Todd feel slightly uncomfortable.

But it was when he started describing his OOB experiences that I found myself spellbound. I had read the celebrated Robert Monroe's pioneering *Journeys Out of the Body*, but here were new ideas I'd never encountered before. I felt energised but also a little apprehensive. Some of what he was saying was so revolutionary I wasn't sure how well it meshed with the neat little framework I'd spent years putting together, which wrapped me in its cosy cocoon just like a comfort blanket.

Then a wonderful synchronicity occurred. Someone mentioned I was the 'famous author' Ian Lawton – something of an exaggeration but never mind – at which Todd strode out of the room and returned carrying his rucksack. 'Well how d'ya like that?' he beamed, pulling out a copy of my *Wisdom of the Soul*. 'I was searching my shelf for a book to read on the train, and this just jumped out at me! I've had it for some time but never picked it up before.' After what I'd already heard from him I was none too sure that my previous use of the word *wisdom* was appropriate, but he politely waved away my concerns and we became firm friends from that moment.

We agreed to meet in a pub in central London a few weeks later so we could talk some more. As he drew diagrams on scraps of paper about the different planes of our 'human hologram', and so on and so forth, I began to feel like a beginner again – not least because, instead of just *theorising* about them as I did, he'd actually *visited* them and experimented in each. Despite my concerns about my newly discovered limitations, he even invited me to speak at one of his weekend OOB workshops. I agreed provided he let me attend the whole event.

It was a fascinating experience, but I didn't manage to get OOB then or during the month of regular practice that followed. I think it was through a combination of shame that I'd given up so easily, and of fear that much of what I thought I knew might need to be revisited, that Todd and I lost touch after this. I received occasional mailings from him, and sometimes replied to congratulate him on the way his Journey of Truth 'meetup' group in London was expanding and achieving wonderful things on the ground. He had hordes of people meditating and manifesting all over London, and they were clearly having huge fun into the bargain.

In fact, because I'd been going through my ever-worsening dark night of the soul more or less since we met, it was all I could manage not to be jealous. Finally I emailed Todd to get his views on our conflicting experiences, and he immediately replied that he'd get down to see me as soon as possible, which was extremely kind. As it turned out he struggled to make it to the wilds of North Dorset, but he encouraged me to visit him in London. I was still apprehensive. I knew we'd be bound to start talking spiritual frameworks again, and that there was a good possibility I'd have to massively alter my own.

Around this time I was visiting another friend from the therapy world for some shamanic energy clearance, and she convinced me I needed to pick up the baton again and face my fears. Thank heavens Louise had the foresight and intuition to push me in such an important direction.

I had pretty much brushed my previous discussions with Todd under the carpet in the intervening eighteen months, but now I dusted off the list of questions I'd prepared for him after our initial meetings. I tweaked them to allow for certain things I'd learned in the meantime, and then I was off to London. I had been forced to sell my 500 Honda when my finances got tight, but I'd recently been able to replace it with a classic 750 Honda that I'd bought as a bit of a wreck and rebuilt, again as a cracking-looking café racer but this time all in black and gold.

I arrived at Todd's flat with eyes on stalks from negotiating London traffic on a bike for the first time ever. Unabashed he immediately thrust me under his newly acquired 'lucid light' machine, despite my protestations that I was quite spaced out enough already. Nevertheless it was an interesting experience and we soon found ourselves relaxing in each other's company as if there had been no interlude. That is when we went out for a curry, and my big shock became inescapable.

So why is Todd's experience of another, far wiser aspect of himself so crucial that it's forcing me to reappraise my whole spiritual framework?

In simple terms, Rational Spirituality is based on a traditional view of reincarnation – that is, we lead many and varied lives one *after* the other. At the same time the theory has it that we have a so-called 'higher self' that effectively remains in the higher planes while we incarnate on earth. So between each life, in the interlife, the experiences of the life just lived are assimilated by the higher self, and plans are made for the next life that will hopefully provide an opportunity for 'soul growth'. The higher self, or soul if you prefer, is therefore always growing towards some point of wisdom or enlightenment or whatever you want to call it whereby it no longer needs the experience of incarnating on the Earth plane, and can move on to other things.

But the entity that Todd is describing as his oversoul, Acamesis, clearly represents a very different level of consciousness from this. It is *already* incredibly wise and powerful, even divine or godlike. Yet it's still very much an individual entity, so he definitely isn't describing some sort of universal Source. Nothing in interlife research even remotely resembles such an entity.

Bear in mind that for many years I've been able to reasonably lay claim to being the world's foremost expert in this line of research. Not only that but when I completed my past-life regression training I went on to learn the additional techniques for taking people into the deeper state of hypnosis required to guide them into the interlife, and have practised this with quite a few clients. But the truth now has to be faced, which is that for some time my interlife sessions – both as subject and as therapist – have been creating increasingly nagging doubts about the validity of using this type of research as a key source of evidence for my spiritual worldview.

To be clear, there's no doubt that as the main pioneer Newton moved our understanding forward by bringing the interlife experience generally, and the idea of responsibility for our own life planning in particular, to the awareness of literally tens of thousands of people – not least myself. However he also produced something of a blueprint for the experience that was far more detailed than anything that had gone before, especially in his second book.

Although he never released full case details or transcripts of session recordings, I've come to realise from personal experience that almost certainly he must have been *leading* some if not most of his subjects to follow this blueprint far more than I'd previously appreciated. The same may be true of some, even many, of those who trained under him. Whereas my own observation, and that of many of my contemporaries, is that the interlife experience is far, far more fluid and varied than a reader of Newton's work would appreciate.

Moreover there's another problem. It has always troubled me that, following the example of my good friend Andy Tomlinson, I and others have always maintained that the interlife experience effectively takes place in what we term the 'eternal now'. Yet in truth this has always been diametrically opposed to the traditional concept of reincarnation – and we've always tended to just sweep this contradiction under the carpet. But no longer.

To understand and face this contradiction head on we need to delve into some concepts that are incredibly hard for any of us to really grasp as human beings – so hang on to your hats! In simple terms, for millennia spiritual and esoteric sources have been telling us that 'time' is only a perception that we humans use while on the Earth plane to allow our limited brains to process what is going on, and to make sense of the experience.

In other words, *consecutive* time that appears to flow *from* the past, *through* the present and *into* the future is just an illusion. As the great Eckhart Tolle so elegantly puts it in *The Power of Now*, the apparent past is no longer happening and the apparent future hasn't happened yet, so *now* is all that exists. Over time I develop a way of trying to describe this by suggesting that time is a 'discrete series of now moments'.

Now even though I've contemplated this idea for some years I don't claim for one moment to fully understand *how* it really works. But what I do decide is that, since my entire worldview is being ripped apart anyway, it's about time someone took it seriously instead of only paying it lip service.

The contradiction is of course that if time doesn't really exist – especially in the higher planes – and everything is happening in the now, how on earth can we still place everything in the traditional reincarnatory framework of having many lives one *after* the other? Instead, as hard as it is to grasp, logically it must follow that they must all be happening *at the same time* – irrespective of the era involved. This means that, for example, Big Bill is still alive, and his life is going on alongside mine. Mindblowing! But almost certainly true.

By the way, in case you're thinking that this time I really have lost it, consider this. Mainstream physics has for decades been forced to accept something that runs completely counter-intuitive to human experience. It is that what we perceive as physical matter – tables, chairs, our bodies and so on – is nothing of the sort. It is just waves of energy, or 'quanta'. Although physicists remain far from developing a comprehensive model that can *explain* quantum behaviour, the *fact* of it remains – and there's not a serious scientist in the world who would dispute it. So don't ever be fooled by your perceptions. Reality – whatever that is – is far stranger than you could possibly imagine.

As a result of all this I'm now faced with the task of developing a new spiritual model in which each of us is an 'aspect' of a supremely divine yet individual consciousness, *and* where it is projecting these aspects into different human eras concurrently rather than consecutively. But as if that's not enough, there's yet another problem. The interlife-based worldview I've supported for so long contains yet another inherent contradiction. Although I and many others of like mind have always claimed to believe in the law of attraction – in other words in the idea that we're creating our own experience as we go along – how can this be consistent with the idea of having a life plan that is already broadly established?

I have always got around this conundrum by suggesting that there are greater 'probabilities' and lesser 'possibilities' in our life plans, and that it's within these parameters that we have freedom to create our own experience. But in truth I've always known in my heart that this is a fudge. Just as with concurrent or consecutive lives, I now come to the conclusion that this isn't one of those 'both are true at the same time' paradoxes. I have a strong feeling that I can no longer sit on the fence on these issues. In both cases, it has to be one or the other. Moreover of course they're connected, because if all my lives are simultaneous there can be no such thing as a *next* life plan, and I must be creating my reality in its entirety.

So I am both massively excited and disoriented all at the same time. I am desperately trying to make sense of this new way of looking at things.

Quite what its full implications are I don't know yet. But I do know that I find it increasingly momentous that each of us turns out to be an integral part of a consciousness so wise and so divine, yet at the same time still individualised and personal to each of us – in a way that vague notions of some ultimate Source could never be.

I also know that this – combined with the idea that all lives are happening at the same time, and that each of us is responsible for creating every aspect of our experience – will produce a worldview that will be revolutionary for huge swathes of spiritual seekers weaned, like me, on a diet of traditional reincarnation. How many will be ready to accept such radical ideas – perhaps as part of the shift – and to see their wonderfully transformative potential for the human race?

Over the next few weeks after my fateful meeting with Todd I read Monroe's second and third books, *Far Journeys* and *Ultimate Journey*, which I'd bought after our first few meetings but left on the shelf. As Todd has suggested they're completely different and far more revealing than the first, and they seem to corroborate his experience.

Within three weeks I know I have to write my first entirely new research-based book for more than five years. I also feel strongly that expressions such as *oversoul* and *higher self* already have too many confusing connotations, and that something new is probably required. I wake up one morning with the title *Supersoul* gifted into my consciousness. Those few people I discuss it with seem to love the whole concept.

I know I'm on the right track.

My research for *Supersoul* takes a good twelve months of concentrated work. I collate evidence for its existence from not only a whole host of OOB pioneers who've had similar experiences to Todd, but also from corroborative channelled material from well known ethereal sources such as Jane Roberts' 'Seth' and Neale Donald Walsch's 'God'. The trouble is I also send myself nearly crazy trying to develop several different theoretical models of how the various different levels of soul consciousness might operate and interact, and by the time I publish the first edition I still haven't nailed my colours to the mast as to which one I support.

In fact it's only after another few months of contemplation that I arrive at a proper conclusion, which is partly based on undertaking new research into the afterlife from similar OOB and channelled sources – which as we saw in the opening chapter will ultimately become a book in its own right. What I discover is that all the evidence from these sources seems to point to the individual personality continuing on into the afterlife, and developing from there. There is no mention of merging with some sort of higher self as per the traditional reincarnation model.

This simplifies things considerably. Rather than there being three levels or 'aggregations' of consciousness – the 'life personality', the 'soul' and the 'supersoul' – instead the first two are effectively one and the same. What also becomes clear is that because the collective consciousness of each supersoul is projecting all its myriad aspects into different human lives simultaneously, rather than it growing over time its 'databanks' of experience are constantly being enriched as part of an automatic feedback loop in the eternal now.

As to what levels of consciousness might lie beyond the supersoul, that would obviously be pure speculation. But what all this does suggest is that when people talk of 'experiencing' or 'merging with' Source consciousness itself they're likely to be mistaken. Instead such an experience of 'oneness' is almost certainly achieved when making contact with their own supersoul. But let's remember that there will be many, many individual supersouls just involved with the Earth experience, let alone other realities that might be completely different.

Talking of which, another piece of research I immerse myself in heavily at this time is the work of a man almost uniquely placed to explain all this because he is both a highly qualified physicist *and* a pioneering OOB explorer. Todd recommends Thomas Campbell to me, but I discover that I've actually put a link to his work on my website some years ago and then forgotten about it. His *My Big T.O.E.* – or 'theory of everything' – runs to three volumes and several thousand pages, and isn't an easy read. Yet it's another of those books that has a huge influence on me.

In a nutshell Campbell endorses the view taken by many eminent 20th century physicists: that the evidence of quantum theory only makes sense once we accept that consciousness itself is primal and underlies everything. The corollary is that what we experience as apparently material or physical reality is merely a projection of our consciousness – almost like a film where we are both individually and collectively the directors, and which has no objective validity until we choose to shoot a particular scene.

This acceptance of the primacy of consciousness has unfortunately taken a back seat in recent decades, which is arguably why little real progress has been made in interpreting quantum theory in that time. But with a recent increase in focus on what scientists have dubbed the 'hard problem' of consciousness, all the signs are that it's due for a resurgence – and that the days of the pure materialist really may be numbered.

But Campbell goes further, and again isn't alone in suggesting that what I call supersouls are creating new 'realities', 'universes' or 'holograms' all the time. Further that these may usefully be likened to the most complex simulations in computer games – with all possible moves worked out in advance, although each player still has free will to choose which precise path they navigate through the game.

This means that our own 'human-on-Earth' game would be just one of an almost unlimited number of possible games or realities that supersouls can project aspects of themselves into, and play around in. Indeed the evidence even suggests there are multiple versions of just our own game. This comparison with a game is an extremely useful one in other ways too. It has connotations with us being mere actors who are here to play a part – meaning that, although the game or play is so convincing that we can end up experiencing enormous levels of pleasure and pain, no permanent damage can be done to our underlying consciousness.

Another hugely important question that philosophers have struggled with for millennia is, of course, how do we explain the apparent inequalities in people's lives in terms of abundance or lack of money, love, success and so on? Under the traditional model the answer was that we experience many lives of all different types in successive incarnations. Under our new model the same is true except they're all happening at the same time. Nevertheless it's still clear that each time our supersoul projects an aspect of itself into the Earth game it chooses a set of what I call 'birth givens' for that projection, and these vary widely – in terms not just of our sex but also of our main psychological and physical traits and propensities, and the socio-economic position and geographical location of our parents. This means that our aim as humans, at least once we reach adulthood and are responsible for our own decisions, must be to 'paint the best picture we can with the palette we've been given.'

Eventually I pull all this together into what I finally feel is a coherent model of what I refer to as 'Supersoul Spirituality', and publish it in a second edition of the book.

Just around the time of my key meeting with Todd described in the opening passage, another change occurs. Several years ago when I was living in Westbourne and on one of my jaunts across the water, quite by chance I discovered a beautifully-located campsite just on the other side of the Purbeck Ridge on the outskirts of Swanage. For some reason I had a sense that one day I might want to live at a place like this, so I walked in but was told in no uncertain terms that it was completely full and there was a long waiting list for seasonal or year-round pitches.

I think nothing more of this until one day when Kenny, Pam and I are visiting Swanage for a music festival. It is early afternoon and I ask them if they'll drop me off so I can take a walk up through my old enchanted wood and onto the ridge, not having been there for some time. But instead of returning the same way as I always used to I'm dropping down the other side to walk on into Swanage itself. Lo and behold, as I'm strolling along a narrow country lane at a place called Herston, there's the campsite again! Not only that but when I enter reception the helpful Liz tells me they have plenty of seasonal pitches.

Now by this time my training work seems to be starting to pick up just a little, and in any case I've been at Ken and Pam's for over a year and it's high time I stopped subjecting them to my problems. So Liz shows me what is available, I pick a wonderful spot looking right out onto the ridge, and the deal is done there and then. Although I will be paying monthly rent again, it's a *very* economical way to live.

Having said that this introduces a greater pressure on attracting work so I can pay said rent, and I'm getting desperate again when one day something marvellous happens that truly transforms my life – and will come to represent probably the most important practical aspect of my new worldview. It's all very well knowing the theory, but can I translate it into action?

I am sitting in the Love Bus one afternoon, focussing heavily on new research for *Supersoul*. Time flies when I'm fully engaged like this – I don't stop for refreshments, the toilet or anything for hours on end when I'm totally in the zone. At around 6pm I stop and check my emails, and I'm excited yet petrified when I see that one of the companies who occasionally give me training work is looking for someone to run a week-long course quite soon. The problem is the email arrived around two hours ago.

To explain, the smaller training companies I've been working with will have a few first-choice associates who they've worked with for a long time and who they book in advance. This means when they have an urgent new requirement they send an email to trainers on their second-string list – which is where I still reside – and whoever responds first wins. Normally I check my emails regularly but on this occasion I've been too preoccupied. I immediately fire back a response, actually admitting that I'm desperate for the work and hoping they haven't allocated it to someone else.

It gets to the evening and I'm so nervous I go to the pub. While I'm there the fateful email comes back – they're sorry but they've given the work to someone else. I literally start to go into meltdown. Just one course pays enough that it can transform my life for at least a few months. That is why it's such a case of 'feast and famine' and why I'm absolutely desperate, especially now I have to pay rent again – and I've missed their email by my own stupidity. Why hadn't I switched on email alerts? Just as with the episode with Katherine I can feel panic building and a physical pain developing in my chest – it's almost like a heartbreak again.

Yet suddenly I once more hear a clear voice inside my head: 'Don't panic, Ian. Don't go into victim mode. You have a *choice*... and anyway there is something else for you. Just trust.'

Suddenly it's as if the scales are removed from

my eyes. In a blinding flash of insight it becomes crystal clear to me that all the while I've been going through my dark night I *have* been in victim mode, I just haven't been able to see it. Every time something bad has happened I've had a choice. I could front it up, brush myself off and go again without delay. Or I could curl up in my bed in the foetal position, feel incredibly sorry for myself and act like a victim. And that is what I've consistently chosen to do, especially the worse things have become.

Sometimes I've hidden myself away for several days, sometimes just for a few minutes. But now I understand. Every time I've done that I've reinforced my victim status and, by the law of attraction, made sure more potential victim situations would come my way. It doesn't matter that much of the rest of the time I've been trying to remain positive, visualising positive outcomes and trying out new ways to extricate myself from my plight. The intensity of my feelings of self-pity when I *have* been in victim mode has been over-riding all of that. What is more, I realise that I've actually become *attracted* to my victimhood. It has almost become an unacknowledged badge of honour –

I've actually been *preferring* it to staying strong.

Of course during my dark night I've been repeatedly and desperately trying to work out *why* so many horrid things have been happening to me. I don't believe in any sort of god, or in random chance, while my Rational Spiritual model has never accepted the idea of 'bad karma' passing from one life to another. So all that's been left for me under that model is the idea that, because we plan the challenges we're going to face in each life, I must have *chosen* all these trials to really test myself. Indeed sometimes I've allowed myself to assume that my life plan somehow involves going to extremes of suffering – not the worst ever, of course, but pretty bad – perhaps even so I can teach others something from my experience.

Reality now stares me hard in the face. What total, utter, egotistical nonsense I've been using as an excuse. Nonsense that has prevented me from taking full responsibility for the mess I've been creating.

So despite receiving such bad news I feel strangely refreshed and, while it wouldn't be true to say I fully trust the message that something else is on its way, I am at least open to it. What is more important, I *don't* let myself lapse into victim mode. In fact I swear to myself that never, *ever* again will I allow that to happen, come what may.

The following morning an email comes in from a different company offering several days work. It isn't a full week, but it's an absolute godsend nonetheless. I cannot remember the last time I've received two offers of work in as many days.

Once again my inner voice spoke the truth.

We have seen that for some years now I've understood the whole concept of the law of attraction and of consciously creating outcomes I desire – using the sort of visualisation and other techniques I was automatically practising all those years ago when I was racing, when I'd never read or heard a thing about them. I have had some success with it at least as far back as when I attracted my lovely flat in Westbourne, but clearly it hasn't worked for most of the time I've been in victim mode during my dark night, because I've been sabotaging it. So now I'm coming out of that episode can I start to make it work for me again?

For some time one of my goals has been to meet more like-minded, spiritual people. Now I'm no longer doing therapy work, coupled with the downturn in my writing career, I've lost touch with many of my former friends and colleagues. So once I arrive in Swanage I decide, as a practical way of putting this desire into effect, to make use of the online 'meetup' tool Todd uses to set up what I call the 'Spiritual Exchange'.

The intention is to do something a bit different, in that most spiritual groups tend to invite a speaker along for an evening, whereas I've always preferred open discussions not dominated by any one person. So this will be a discussion group in which all members can join in. I put up posters and fliers in both Swanage and Bournemouth, and I visualise well-attended and enjoyable meetings, and all the friendships that will spring from them.

As it turns out only the Bournemouth group takes off, but at our inaugural meeting nearly twenty people turn up. Better still, when I ask everyone to introduce themselves and we go round the table, they start opening up to complete strangers in the most wonderful and unexpected way – 'coming straight from the heart' as we call it. It sets a wonderful tone and we go on to meet every week, sometimes with topics to discuss arranged in advance, but always with a core group of people who develop strong friendships and bonds.

It is also at our first meeting that I encounter Neil, who tells me that he's just got involved with a group of people who arrange ceremonies to partake in Ayahuasca 'medicine' here in the UK. This is the well-publicised natural hallucinogen used by native Peruvian tribes to induce visionary journeys and self-enlightenment, and I tell him I've always fancied trying it. So it is that not long afterwards I'm lying in his unpretentious living room in suburban Bournemouth, surrounded by fellow journeyers burping and vomiting copiously into buckets for several hours on end throughout the night. It sounds awful, but in fact it's quite wonderful.

Admittedly the medicine itself tastes like shit, and my personal journey isn't overly enlightening – unusually I end up in a fairly paranoid state that I have to work hard to control. But the initial experience of psychedelic colours and shapes all morphing into each other, and the sense that apparently physical reality is crumbling, is hugely interesting and entertaining to someone who has never tried LSD or the like.

Yet what really gives me the most satisfaction, a little like my experience with the therapy training, is the bond that forms between us through that night and into the next morning. You don't share a space like that and not become close – particularly when I hear some of the wonderfully transformative experiences some of the others have had as we do a 'group share' once everyone is more or less restored to this reality.

Of course I'm very much aware that it's illegal to take Ayahuasca in the UK, but that strikes me as absolutely ridiculous given that, as usual, this is based on total and utter ignorance. Studies into the effects of this and other natural hallucinogens have shown remarkable improvements in people suffering from all sorts of psychological disorders – and also, paradoxically, in drug and alcohol addicts. This not least because they tend to be shown their true state while in trance, and it seems to wake them up. That is why those involved insist on calling it *medicine*, and would never use the word *drug*. But I guess 'big pharma' has a huge vested interest in making sure politicians don't provide an alternative to doctors prescribing their anti-depressants in ever-increasing numbers.

I attend several more ceremonies, and the general social scene at festivals and other gatherings in East London is thoroughly enjoyable. But I also see people who I feel allow the medicine to take over their life – for example, ending up allowing 'Mother Aya' to make their choices for them in every area. This is, of course, not for me, because I feel it's just the same as abrogating responsibility for one's experience to a god, or to karma, or whatever. So I gradually drift away, although with fond memories.

Of course I'm now proactively targeting attracting more training work too. The economy is finally turning a bit of a corner, albeit slowly, and I sense that after two lean years the time is ripe for more work to come my way. As is often suggested in books on conscious creation, rather than concentrate on the mechanics of *how* this will come about, instead I focus on the *outcome* itself. I visualise myself teaching groups of people who are learning eagerly, and I focus on the feeling of having plenty of money again to enjoy things I like doing.

Early in 2013 I'm running one of my rare courses and the PRINCE2 governing body take that opportunity to send in an observer to make sure I'm still doing my job properly. This is part of maintaining my qualification, and it needs to happen every couple of years. These observers can tend to be the sort who really need to get out more, but on this occasion Graham is a very friendly chap who seems to like my style of training. In a coffee break I tell him that I'm desperately short of work, and already by that lunchtime he's made a phone call to a contact in another of the UK's leading training companies, QA, to provide me with an introduction.

Just as Andy did originally, Graham literally saves the day. Because this is a much larger company, in no time I have regular work flowing in and I'm out of financial trouble. Of course money isn't the be-all-and-end-all of my life but, when you're up against it in other areas, having the money to buy a couple of pints or a nice meal can make you feel a hell of a lot better.

So not only am I avowedly no longer a victim, I'm now unequivocally proving the reality of consciously creating and directing my experience too.

At least in *some* areas of my life.

2016

the creating never stops

It is early in the year. I have wrapped up warm so I can take a late-night stroll along the beach in Weymouth, where I now live. In my headphones I'm listening to a recording of a fellow researcher talking about the neural pathways in the brain, how they create our perception of 'reality', and how we can retrain them to create any set of experiences we want.

After an hour or so I arrive home in pensive mood. As I walk through the hallway of the Georgian block of flats where I live, I glance in the huge antique mirror... and that's when it hits me.

For several years I've been writing about the fundamental supremacy of the law of attraction. But now, for the first time, I realise there's been a part of me that still hasn't been sure. For a short time I've even managed to attract a partner who clearly mirrors this uncertainty back to me by repeatedly questioning my beliefs: 'If you're creating all this and you want your books to be selling, how come they're not?'

But now, finally, as I stare at myself in the mirror, a deep sense of joy and relief brings tears welling to the surface. The researcher I've been listening to is properly scientifically trained. I speak aloud to my reflection: 'You're *not* mad. You're *not* talking nonsense. This stuff is actually *real*!'

Finally, belief has become knowing.

At the beginning of 2014, at the same time as I was putting together the second edition of *Supersoul*, I was also preparing another book. This came about because some months before, at a meeting of the Spiritual Exchange, one of the regular attendees had tipped me off about two sources of channelled material I hadn't encountered before – Darryl Anka's 'Bashar' and Marry Ennis' 'Elias' – that he thought would be relevant to my research.

The following day I looked up their work online and this more than justified his suggestion. Most revelatory for me, both of them were confirming something I'd been hinting at in my writing but still hadn't fully understood until now. For sure I'd already accepted that it was possible to consciously create desirable outcomes in my life, and also that when this didn't work it was most likely because I was sabotaging said outcomes via my mainly subconscious beliefs – especially when these were connected with obvious victimhood. But what both these sources were unequivocally stating, and what I hadn't properly taken on board prior to this, was that we aren't just creating our reality when we make a conscious effort to do it. Instead we're creating our reality *all the time*. It isn't an optional process. It is automatic. It never switches off.

This was another crucial piece of the jigsaw that I'd been missing. It was the part that finally and fully underpinned my resolve to never, ever be a victim again. Why? Because adopting such a stance becomes simply impossible as soon as we properly accept that we're creating every single aspect of our experience.

Even more important for our current purposes, *this* is this vital piece of understanding that forced me to write this book when confronted with the idea that people were rejecting the law of attraction en masse as something that 'doesn't work', as described in the opening chapter. Why? Because that statement can now be seen to be a complete nonsense. Whether or not you properly understand its workings, you can't turn away from an all-pervasive law that underpins our experience as fundamentally as breathing!

Having opened up this line of thinking I started to look into what other well-known channelled sources had to say on the matter. These included not only Jane Roberts' 'Seth' and Neale Donald Walsch's 'God' who I'd used in my research for *Supersoul*, but also Eva Pierrakos' 'Pathwork Guide', JZ Knight's 'Ramtha', Esther Hicks' 'Abraham', and Jayem's 'Jeshua' from *The Way of Mastery*. I guess I shouldn't have been surprised that they were *all* confirming exactly this point: that however much it may appear that things are happening *to* us in this powerful illusion we call being human on Earth, in fact our own thoughts, beliefs, preconceptions, conditioning, expectations and so on will have been responsible for every single thing we experience, *with no exceptions*.

Now, of course, even people who've heard of the law of attraction tend to baulk at this suggestion when they're first presented with it. 'But we're interacting with other human beings!' they cry. 'So if my girlfriend leaves me for no good reason, or I lose my job because of cost cuts, there's no way I've *created* that situation myself. These are *other people's* decisions.' But what these wise sources insist we have to come to terms with is there are *no* exceptions. Whatever the situation, somewhere along the line our own thoughts, beliefs and so on have created it, or perhaps more accurately *attracted* it into our life. No matter how major or minor, no matter how obvious or obscure the underlying dynamics and linkages.

A good example of all this is that it's becoming increasingly accepted in the modern world that many apparently physical illnesses actually stem from emotional dis-ease. The only difference is that our channelled sources would substitute the word *all* for *many*. Moreover, looking at things the other way around, for several decades now pioneering studies have been producing a huge amount of evidence to support the notion of the 'placebo effect'. For example, people with back or shoulder pain have had operations that completely mirrored the real thing except once the surgeons were inside the body they did nothing – yet significant numbers of patients subsequently reported a lessening or complete cessation of pain.

On a more purely mental level, track cyclists were given a new, supposedly performance-enhancing pill made only from cornflower, and every single one improved their times. Students suffering from relationship heartbreak were given a supposedly analgesic nasal spray that contained a weak saline solution, and a significant number reported feeling better about their ex-partner.

Perhaps best of all, a large, recent UK study saw 117 people in Blackpool, who had suffered severe back pain often for more than a decade, take a 'new' painkiller. Crucial was that they believed in the authenticity of the whole programme, so the researchers set up a pretend medical clinic with real doctors and proper consultations, the pills needed to look authentic, the bottle had all the usual stuff on the label and so on. After three weeks more than half felt their pain had lessened considerably or completely gone. Best of all the effect continued in many of them even after they were told they'd only taken a placebo.

On top of anecdotal evidence of mother's using superhuman strength to lift cars off trapped children, this is now providing us with proper, scientific studies of the power of mind over matter… or, to put it another way, of how our thoughts and beliefs condition our experience.

As a rider to all this though, even if we perhaps understandably refuse to accept that we ourselves have created or attracted a hugely challenging situation into our lives – such as major illness afflicting ourselves or others close to us, or even the death of a loved one – then at the very least we should be prepared to take full responsibility for how we *react* to said situation.

I am fully aware that the idea that we're personally responsible for creating or attracting every single experience in our lives at best takes a hell of a lot of digestion. More likely many of you will be inclined to simply reject it, partly because of the apparent starkness of the message, and partly because it doesn't seem intuitively likely that we can be creating or attracting every single experience when we're interacting so much with others. So, despite the consistency of our channelled sources' message, and the evidence of the placebo effect, is there any other hard evidence to back it up? Indeed there is, and again it comes from my research into the afterlife.

In particular OOB explorers and channelled sources all agree that in the higher vibratory realms thoughts and expectations instantly translate into reality. So if you want to see a dead relative... hey presto! Just think of them and they're instantly with you or you with them. Similarly, if your expectation of heaven is a deserted cottage on a windswept moor, or a beautiful sandy beach with pristine white sand and turquoise water, or a religious congregation who still worship exactly the same as they did on Earth... da da! Just having that expectation will create it, or attract you to an environment where others have already created it for you.

The impeccable logic then runs that exactly the same is true of our human experience on Earth, except that here we're much more under the influence of space-time. So, for example, in this plane we actually have to walk or use some sort of transport to be in each other's presence, instead of just thinking it. This means there's usually a noticeable delay between a thought and its manifestation in our reality. This effect is exacerbated by this being a 'consensus' or shared reality, in which our own thoughts and intentions are mingling and sometimes competing with those of our fellows around us. This means the link between thought and manifested result is usually even more difficult to trace, sometimes even impossible with our limited human understanding. But it's always there.

Of course this state of affairs is accurately expressed in age-old axioms such as 'What goes around comes around,' 'You reap what you sow,' and various others. But it's all too easy to shy away from the fact that this is happening *all the time*. Our perceived reality is *always* just a mirror accurately reflecting our thoughts and beliefs back to us. Just *how* it does this – so that every single person in a complex interaction is still experiencing *exactly* what they've attracted to themselves as an individual – is way beyond our human understanding. But the fact that somehow it *does* do this should perhaps no longer be in question.

So what are the further implications of the all-pervasive law of attraction? A huge one is that, to the extent that we're not creating our reality consciously, we're doing it *un*consciously. In other words our subconscious beliefs, programming and so on are taking over, to create an experience that matches those often limiting beliefs and trapped, unhelpful emotions that can build up both in childhood and then all the way through our lives.

That is why it's so important to attempt to unearth and release these repressed emotions, and to reprogram the associated beliefs, if we're to lead the full and abundant lives we each deserve. Otherwise they will continually exert an unwanted, usually hidden influence that can prevent us from creating the outcomes we most desire. We may even need the help of professional therapists or counsellors to achieve this – and that's not an admission of defeat or a sign of weakness.

It is also why it's important to cultivate the 'observer self' who can be constantly on the look out for such mainly hidden beliefs making themselves known in the language we use – in phrases such as 'I always struggle with money' or 'partners always treat me badly then leave.' If we have observant friends we can ask them to point out whenever we're expressing such limiting beliefs but, with practice, we can learn to spot them for ourselves – whether in our spoken words or merely in our thoughts.

So what we should be aiming for is to maximise the extent to which we're consciously rather than unconsciously creating our experience. As to the nature of the outcomes we can consciously create for ourselves, actually the sky is the limit. We can create literally *anything* we desire, provided our belief in it is strong enough and it's not being hampered by our subconscious. All sources suggest that in theory at least 'the universe' makes no distinction between manifesting a parking space – which, by the way, is the nice, simple example we all tend to use as beginners to prove the process works – and manifesting a huge mansion. Nevertheless, most people do tend to start small and work their way up.

Of course, because all this new understanding was such a crucial piece of the jigsaw for Supersoul Spirituality, I felt it deserved its own book. So the second volume in the 'Supersoul Series' was born, and by the middle of 2014 *The Power of You* was complete.

Again I published it myself. I had approached other companies while writing *Supersoul*, and a few had shown some interest. But the industry was by now in such a financially precarious position – what with competition from e-books and so on – that for a proposal to be accepted you either had to be a well-established author with a huge, self-generated, social-media following, or your idea had to be so revolutionary or eye-catching that they took a chance on it. I felt the concept of the supersoul easily fitted the latter bill, but what did I know?

Having been single for some time, in the summer of 2014 I met a lovely woman at a small music festival in the grounds of Sherborne Castle. I liked her, and she liked me, and since I'd still never been married I thought it was high time I should be. Ever the impetuous risk taker I proposed after only six weeks, taking a chilled bottle of champagne and two glasses in a rucksack to the place where we first met and getting down on one knee. Lilly gleefully accepted, but unfortunately our relationship went pretty much downhill from that moment onwards.

Yet this didn't stop me perhaps foolishly accepting when she asked me to come and live with her and her three teenage children in a beautiful converted barn in a small hamlet north of Sherborne – and at the same time giving up my pitch on the camp site and selling the Love Bus. Silly boy.

For about a month things were perfect, but then the arguments started. My tax affairs had been somewhat haphazard for a number of years, not least because there were long periods when I wasn't earning enough to pay any. So I'd basically flown under the radar because, when money was tight, rather than claim benefits from the government I would borrow from friends knowing that I'd pay them back when things picked up – which I always did. In that way I didn't feel I was cheating anyone.

But now she broke it to me that her ex-husband was a very vindictive and wealthy man who was likely to employ someone to pry into my personal affairs and dig up whatever dirt he could find. So not only did she suggest I needed to get my tax affairs sorted out, but she also insisted I needed to rent a flat of my own with my own address so it didn't look like I was living with her. Of course I wondered why she hadn't come out with all this *before* she asked me to move in.

By this time I could afford to rent again, but my plan had been to carry on living cheaply in the bus while I paid off my debts. So now not only had all that flown out the window, but I was also coming clean to the tax authorities and arranging to pay them a not-insignificant sum in back tax. I took this with as much good grace as I could, and in hindsight she probably did me a favour, but at the time I wasn't best pleased.

We decided that because Sherborne had no night life I should rent a flat in Weymouth, a place I'd loved for some time anyway. The plan was for it to be my official residence and a weekend getaway for the two of us. When the estate agent mentioned a flat in Gloucester Lodge, which hadn't yet been officially put on the rental market because it was being decorated, I immediately recognised the name but couldn't think where from.

We went to see it from the outside and it was a beautiful, Georgian, ex-hotel right on The Esplanade, opposite the beach. It hardly needed us to look inside several days later and see the beautiful views across the bay from the two large windows in the wonderfully light and spacious living room. Once again I'd hit the jackpot in terms of finding somewhere special to live and being the first person to view it – and, yes, an element of conscious creation and visualisation was again involved.

It was only a few days later that I realised where I recognised the name from. For some years I'd made a habit of reading and re-reading the complete works of both Charles Dickens and Thomas Hardy. For me it was pure escapism from the current world, although the similarities in people's behaviour down the ages always fascinated me too. In any case, not long before I'd been reading Hardy's *The Trumpet Major*, set in a small hamlet just north of Weymouth. It depicted how George III and his entire entourage decamped to the seaside town every summer, followed it seems by the entire gentry from across the country – and Gloucester Lodge was his holiday residence. For all I knew my bedroom could have been his!

Despite this fortuitous development my relationship with Lilly was deteriorating. It isn't appropriate for me to go into the reasons except to observe that, while we all have emotional baggage by the time we reach middle age, the hugely important thing is that we should own it and even try to resolve it – sometimes with help from a professional. What we absolutely should *not* do is project it onto our partner. Then again perhaps I pushed a little too hard for certain things to be resolved. In any case, after a final bust-up on Boxing Day I found myself alone in a new town, knowing no one.

Luckily though it wasn't long before I met a great bunch of people through a social meetup group, and we had a lot of fun. I spoilt it though by falling badly for a beautiful local woman pretty much from the moment I saw her – despite warnings both from mutual friends and my own intuition that she was perhaps best avoided. I ignored the lot and jumped in with both feet. Again for about six weeks it was wonderful, and at the end of that time during a weekend away Audrey asked *me* to marry *her*. But luckily I was wary of my recent experience, and politely brushed the issue under the carpet.

Of course once the problems really started we'd both allowed ourselves to become too emotionally committed to back out easily, and we rumbled on with regular, huge bust-ups. We were both desperate to rediscover that intense feeling of togetherness we'd originally shared, but it wasn't going to happen. After six months our break up was inevitably acrimonious, especially as she started to see someone else almost immediately. Having moved around so much in my life I'd rarely dated women local to where I lived – except perhaps in London, and that's a mighty big place. Having to see her with a new man wasn't something I was used to, and I found it a real challenge, but I 'manned up' as best I could.

In the meantime I'd been persuaded to put the various diagrams I use on my training courses into a little book called *PRINCE2 Made Simple*. I even set up my own limited company and for a while tried to market my own courses, gaining full accreditation as a training organisation and so on. I put hundreds of hours into preparing first-rate training materials. What is more I knew that the greatest risk to anyone picking a training provider is the quality of the individual trainer they'll get, which can be pretty variable. So I figured that advertising courses that were guaranteed to be taught by the author of a well-regarded book with a great track record in exam passes and so on ought to be a dead cert.

Unfortunately I'd massively underestimated the competition in the market. I was spending £1500 per month on a Google AdWords campaign, and it was getting me plenty of clicks on my site, but it was producing exactly zero enquiries. It felt like my spiritual workshops all over again. I had one of the best Google analysts working with me, I completely redesigned my website, and we made absolutely sure the ads couldn't be confused for something to do with Prince the musician or by people looking for online instead of classroom courses – all to no avail.

The analyst was as baffled as I was. The only sensible explanation was that other companies were actually employing people to click on rival's adverts to use up their daily budget, which would certainly explain why they only ever reached my home page and stopped there. I have since had this explanation pretty much confirmed by someone in the know. Disgusting.

After several months of haemorrhaging money I had to pull the plug. By this time I'd also found out just how much discounting went on, which meant my attempts to charge at the top end of the spectrum for a high quality service would only work with people who weren't particularly cost conscious. Something else I probably could have foreseen was that large companies want to choose a provider for *all* their training needs, whereas I specialised in project management only. So I accepted that I was fine as I was running courses on behalf of someone else, without all the hassle. But the book I'd written would go on to sell in healthy numbers. If only my spiritual books could even get close!

Talking of which, even as I was moving into Weymouth I was thinking of simpler ways to put across the message of Supersoul Spirituality, rather as I'd done previously by producing pocket books about Rational Spirituality. One thought that had been increasingly growing on me was the whole issue of who Jesus really was and, if he really had existed and performed even half the miracles attributed to him, what had really been going on?

In fact all this came to a head just before Lilly and I split. The tiny church serving the hamlet where she lived was located right next to her front lawn, and we were very much expected to attend the Christmas morning service. I had been in plenty of churches over the years –

actually I always find their atmosphere of still calm a refreshing contrast to the hustle and bustle of the outside world. But I hadn't been in an actual church *service* for decades.

We were of course the last to arrive, having been held up by several bottles of Bucks Fizz, and as we hurried in the only seats available were on the front pew. I actually felt very proud of my 'family' – I got on well with all Lilly's children – and had put on a tweed jacket and shirt to try to look the part of the country gent. But as the service started I found myself sitting right under the nose of the vicar, and began to feel uncomfortable. As we progressed to prayers and hymns, all I could hear was people professing to being weak, sin-filled creatures who needed to be rescued by the tender mercy and love of God and Jesus.

Again I don't for one moment want to disparage the comfort that Christian faith has given to millions of people down the ages, and still does. But the honest truth is this kind of talk started to make me feel physically sick. It was so diametrically opposed to the central message of Supersoul Spirituality – that each of us is an immensely powerful creator god who is entirely responsible for our experience of the world. It was all I could do to get to the end of the service without excusing myself. But when I came out I vowed that never again would I subject myself to such depressing nonsense.

This spurred me on to research Jesus' life and a possible different interpretation thereof. It had been a long time since I read the main New Testament gospels at school, but now I found myself picking out all the key miracles and showing how they could easily be interpreted as him trying to show his disciples and others that they too could perform miracles – or in more modern parlance manipulate apparently physical reality – if only they believed enough in what they were doing.

Consider exhortations such as 'Oh ye of little faith', and 'If you had but the faith of a mustard seed you could move mountains!' Replace the word *faith* with *belief* – in the true nonphysical nature of reality and in our inherent creative power – and my reinterpretation stands up pretty well.

The corollary to all this is that he was insisting there was nothing special about him, and that each and every one of us has the capability to do what he did. If I'm right, how tragic is it that for two millennia we've allowed ourselves to not only miss the point, but to turn it completely on its head? It would mean that the fundamentals of Christian belief are an absolute travesty of the original message. This is certainly what I was feeling in that church.

Now one of the big problems with any of the ancient sacred texts is the extent to which they've been edited over the millennia. Often this has been done far more with political rather than spiritual motives, and this is perhaps particularly true of the Bible. For example, it's now pretty widely accepted that the crucial role Mary Magdalene played in Jesus' life was almost completely edited out by the patriarchal Early Church. Another fascinating fact is that when you study the ancient Mesopotamian texts as I have you find that the story of Noah and the flood is several millennia older than the first editions of the Old Testament.

On top of this the translation of these texts into other languages only serves to further confuse the issue. But my contention is that *if* they retain any validity at all then, in the light of modern scientific discoveries, my reinterpretation of Jesus's message and mission is an entirely reasonable one. What is more, even if they don't, perhaps my reinterpretation provides a timely message for humanity anyway?

My research was held up by the foray into setting up my own training company in the summer, but by the end of 2015 *What Jesus Was Really Saying* was complete and again self-published.

Almost immediately after this I start work on a companion volume that will act as a simple introduction to Supersoul Spirituality generally, partly encouraged by the events narrated in the opening passage. In large part I'm only repeating messages included in *Supersoul* and *The Power of You* in simpler terms. But in addition one of my main objectives this time is to allow people to profit from my own experience, when throughout my dark night I was a victim without even recognising it. Most important, it was my belief in a relatively traditional version of reincarnation that permitted me to think this way because, as I said earlier, I egotistically allowed myself to assume I'd chosen a really challenging life plan.

But I also recognise that people come up with many other excuses that allow them to avoid taking responsibility for the undesirable things they experience. Indeed these are built into most religious and spiritual frameworks. They range from a materialist possibly blaming sheer bad luck and random chance, to a Christian or Muslim saying it's God's or Allah's will, to a Hindu blaming their past-life karma, to a modern reincarnationist perhaps blaming their life plan as I once did.

What I'm about to say may sound somewhat disparaging of other people's views, but I can't help but talk plainly because I believe strongly that that is what's required. A great many people bang the drum about how all religions are basically the same if you boil them down to basics. I don't believe that's true anyway but, if it is, the one thing they do tend to have in common is a mechanism for handing responsibility for what happens in one's life over to someone or something else. I know that not all religious or spiritual people use their faith in that way, but I'm pretty sure many do.

By contrast I feel incredibly strongly that, at the start of the twenty-first century, it's high time the human race set aside these childish superstitions based on centuries-old manuscripts that have in any case been hugely edited for political purposes. We have a plethora of relatively modern evidence from a number of areas of research that give us the chance to paint a far more accurate spiritual picture than we've ever been able to before. We should make use of this chance, and then give our findings some real prominence so that people can consider them for themselves.

Unfortunately when confronted with a moral issue in the news, the default position of the mainstream media remains that they solely elicit the views of atheists and of traditional religious leaders, sometimes organising debates between them. They don't even seem to be aware that a more rational, generally spiritual viewpoint exists and is attracting increasing support. I know this from experience. Some years ago I kept submitting comment articles based on a broad spiritual viewpoint to the mainstream newspapers whenever such an issue raised its head, again to no avail. Only one, *The Guardian*, took me at all seriously, but they just couldn't bring themselves to take the plunge. Maybe the upheaval of social media and online news is changing things, but if so it's still a slow process.

In any case in writing this new, simple book I'm even more keen to promote the idea that each of us is a powerful creator god in our own right – just as I have in *What Jesus Was Really Saying* but from a different perspective. Now, as we saw in the second chapter, probably the best mainstream advert for *conscious* creation or deliberate manifestation is the fact that nearly all top sportspeople now employ a psychologist to help them stay in the moment and visualise success. With the same levels of equipment and talent, the person with the greatest belief will invariably win. This *proves* beyond any shadow of a doubt that conscious creation isn't a figment of my or anyone else's imagination. It is a cold, hard fact. What is more, just because we don't always make it work to our satisfaction does nothing to alter that fact.

On top of that we have all the modern evidence about the placebo effect discussed in the last chapter. This clearly shows, for example, how our *sub*conscious can be fooled into thinking we're taking a painkiller and as a result produce exactly that effect. In other words, it is indisputably shaping the reality we experience.

So another key focus of the new book is to ask what I now see as the 'million dollar' question. If you accept that conscious creation is a reality, as you surely must based on the modern evidence, what else do you think is going on the rest of the time – when undesirable things happen, for example? What logical, spiritual model can you present to me that allows you to be creating *some* of your reality but not *all* of it? I have yet to hear any sort of philosophically elegant answer to this question from the many people with whom I've debated it.

Of course many especially Eastern schools of thought advocate the idea of 'surrender to the flow'. So is there something in this idea that can help to answer my question? One thing of which there can be no doubt is that there can be times when our attempts at conscious creation resemble banging our head against a brick wall. At such times it may well be that something in our subconscious is blocking us, or that the undue intensity of our desire for the outcome – or perhaps for it to be achieved in a particular way – is actually acting as a constraint on the manifestation process rather than aiding it. So in these situations we're better off taking a step back while we work out what's going on – or perhaps even abandoning the pursuit of that outcome for good. This is a form of surrender.

But most followers of Eastern approaches tend to advocate surrender *all* the time, and therefore don't attempt to consciously create at all. The key question then is, who or what is dictating the experience they have? Again is it some sort of god or life plan? Or is that person still creating and attracting their own experience as they drift along through life, albeit almost completely unconsciously? Of course I would answer the latter, and we can use a couple of extreme examples to illustrate how I believe such surrender works.

First, let's consider someone who has had the fortune to be born with a relatively advantageous set of birth givens, and who as a result hasn't developed too many limiting beliefs along the way. Let us say they have a loving, financially comfortable childhood, then meet their soul mate in their late teens, get married early and have a wonderful family that they bring up in exemplary fashion, as their parents did them. They also attract excellent jobs that are fulfilling and pay well too. They have the perfect life, and seem to be able to flow through it – or effectively surrender – without having to put in any great effort. This is of course relatively rare, at least for any prolonged period of time, but we've all encountered the occasional couple who at least *seem* to fall into this category – and we've probably felt a twinge of envy into the bargain.

More common is the situation where a person becomes sufficiently successful in their job, or in their romantic life, or whatever it might be, that at least in that area of their life they have very little if any subconscious blockages preventing them from continued success. So again they can just relax and apparently surrender, at least in those areas. But what's really going on is their subconscious confidence in said areas is actually creating or attracting that continued success, unhindered by limiting beliefs.

But for most of us our lives involve greater and lesser challenges that derive either from our birth givens or are self-created as adults. So, whether we call it conscious creation or not, most of us have to spend time making decisions, and taking resulting actions, that are deliberate attempts to steer our life in a particular direction – that is, *not* just surrendering. What is more, if we *don't* attempt to exercise some degree of proactive control our lives can easily spiral downwards.

To see this, let's take an example at the other extreme – someone who finds themselves living on the street and sleeping rough. This may be due to an especially unfortunate set of birth givens that has almost inexorably led them to this position relatively young in life, while others may have contributed rather more to their situation by their adult choices and so on. I can't think of a better example of complete surrender. Now for a minority this may feel like a total release, and they'll actually enjoy the freedom of the experience despite its evident hardships. But most are leading a wretched, miserable life of dependence and victimhood.

Can their total surrender really be said to be working well for them? Surely it's only when they decide to become proactive, to avail themselves of some of the albeit-limited help available, perhaps most important of all to turn their mindset away from victimhood, that their experience will improve?

Please don't think I'm suggesting this is easy in practice, because many such unfortunates have serious psychological issues. Nor can I ignore the fact that, with far more life advantages, I myself struggled with victimhood and with turning myself away from it. Nor am I advocating not giving such people assistance, in fact quite the reverse, and I certainly wouldn't judge them for the situation they find themselves in – after all we can never know exactly what has led someone else into any given state unless we've walked their precise path, which we never have. But I still maintain that any catalyst for change must always commence within ourselves, with our own attitudes and beliefs.

Within a few months this new book too is ready, and I cannot help but pick the deliberately controversial title... *Sh*t Doesn't Just Happen!!*

2017

endgame

Summer, Donington Park. The rain is beating down with increasing ferocity, and the circuit is awash with water. After qualifying well down the order in dry conditions in an underpowered car, I'm fighting my way up through the field. But this guy is stubborn – and dangerous.

I am getting far better drive out of Redgate Corner, but I can only start to poke my nose up the inside of him as we get to the left-hander at the top of Craner Curves. It is fourth gear, adverse camber, there's a danger of aquaplaning, and for two laps in a row I have to bang my brakes on momentarily as he cuts right across my nose at the last minute. I am very lucky the car doesn't lose traction completely and take us both spinning off onto the grass at speed.

I am racing inches from his back bumper in conditions as bad as I've ever faced in my career. Unbelievably it feels like I've never been away, although in fact I haven't been on a race circuit at all for twenty-two years. Finally I dispatch him and set off after the next group, having been badly held up. By the end of the race I'm on the tail of the group dicing for fourth place, but I've run out of time.

All in all, not a bad comeback for an old bastard.

At the start of 2016 I was beginning to think about leaving Weymouth. As much as I loved it and had some good friends there, having lived in provincial coastal towns for over a decade I was feeling the time might be right for a move back to the more cosmopolitan environment of a city.

I knew I could never live in London again – I enjoyed my time there but it wouldn't suit me now – while to move back to Brighton would be taking me too far over the other side of the south coast, away from friends and family. The one place I'd always heard good things about but never properly experienced was Bristol. So when a course came up there in April I decided to wait 'til I got there then see what sort of rentals might be about.

By the middle of that week I was being shown round a small two-bedroom flat in the heart of the uber-trendy Clifton Village and, despite it being occupied by a doctor who'd left it looking like a bomb had hit it, I was pretty sure it had potential. It felt like a big risk – moving to a new location always does – but I took it all the same.

I loved my time in Bristol, and again met some wonderful people, but I have to say the nightlife and partying was enough to tax the strongest of constitutions. What is more I knew that where there'd been so much upheaval in my life I hadn't been thinking very long term – it was sort of, 'Sod it, let the future look after itself.' But after about six months in Bristol I decided that I needed to think about the future and about saving some money, instead of spending so much on rent when I was working away from home so much anyway. It is such a waste to be paying to leave a flat empty at least half the time. I wasn't keen on sub-letting a room or going back to sharing, so the idea of living in a bus returned. In fact it returned strongly.

I decided that I'd need something bigger than my old Love Bus if I was to be really make myself comfortable, so I found an ex-library bus that looked just the job. Equally fortuitously, after many phonecalls I located a small campsite right on the outskirts of Bath that would let me live there pretty much all the time subject to a few restrictions. Bath is an equally lovely city in a different way, so I had the New Love Bus delivered and set about converting it.

This was a much bigger deal than the original. I started by stripping out all the shelving and heater ducts around the base of the walls, then used pine cladding on the walls as before – but this was a far larger space to cover. With no proper user manual for such a non-standard vehicle the electrics were a complete mystery to me, as well as to the supposed caravan and motorhome expert I paid to come and look at them. So in the end I again had to use my own limited knowledge and logic to rip out much of what was there and start again in a simpler way.

This time the bus had no plumbing either, so I had to build both a kitchen with sink, hob and cupboards, and a separate toilet-cum-shower, from scratch. To get water to them I had to install a water tank, pump and, worst of all, piping to both outlets and to the flush on the electric toilet. This meant lying on wet, muddy ground in the middle of winter, freezing cold, trying to thread pipes and insulation underneath the bus while years of undisturbed mud fell into my eyes. Not pleasant.

But again once it was finished I was proud of my efforts, and with a fully fitted carpet throughout and expensive bespoke cushions for the sofa-cum-spare bed I'd also built, it looked terrific. It was topped off by my beautiful four-poster bed, acquired from eBay when I moved to Weymouth. Despite my supposedly careful measurement it needed several inches cutting off the legs to allow it to fit, this coming on top of the several inches I'd had to cut off the top corners when I moved into the flat in Clifton. But it still looked great, especially when matched with my Corby trouser press. Any self-respecting gentleman should have one, whether living in a bus or not.

Like Bristol and Weymouth, Bath is lovely and holds multiple charms. It is also not far from Castle Combe race circuit, and it's on a trip there on a bank holiday Monday that I watch a couple of races in the MG Owners Club series. It looks like fun, and I feel that having some sort of competition and adrenalin rush again would be good for me. I know I'm supposed to be saving money for the long term but you've got to live as well, otherwise you're just counting off the days. Yes, I realise and accept that I'm guilty of being somewhat inconsistent at times. I just put it down to being in touch with my feminine side.

Such a return will also give me a good reason to lose a bit of weight by cutting down on the excessive food and drink intake, which I've used regularly for a while now as an emotional comfort.

So back in the pits I go and have a chat with Kev, the guy who prepares a number of the front-running cars. Purchase and running costs don't sound prohibitive, so I ask him to keep an eye out for any that are coming up for sale. It is not long before he comes back to me with what sounds like an excellent car for a good price. Unfortunately we suffer several months of delays while it's supposedly being finished off, then when it's finally delivered to him it's a heap of junk. But it's only a week before Donington, a race I really want to do, and we're offered it for a much lower price, so we buy it and Kev goes to work. After the first race described in the opening passage, the second in the dry is far less successful because the engine is well down on power.

Worse still about a month later the car is written off in a startline incident – not my fault – in only my second meeting back. I ask myself if the universe is trying to tell me something, but then

I remember I'm creating all this. For the life of me I can't work out why or how I've manifested the situation, but I just accept that I have and let it go. I must take my own medicine, after all.

As for Bath, lovely as it is I'm struggling to meet people. What is more the old hankering for the Purbeck coast and countryside is coming back. By the Autumn I find myself asking Liz at Herston campsite if she has any space for a larger bus, and although they're pretty much full she kindly finds me a pitch. Although it's by no means as nice as my old one, it gets me back by the coast, which is what I really want.

But, as if I haven't moved around enough over the last two decades, I haven't been back in Swanage long before I walk past a mortgage brokers in the centre of town and, on the spur of the moment, decide to go in. I have briefly investigated getting a mortgage several years ago, and found that the numbers didn't really seem to stack up. After all I need a pretty short mortgage term given my age, which restricts what I can sensibly borrow – and I certainly don't want to live in a box in a crummy place just to satisfy my sister Pam's constant insistence that I should own my own home.

Moreover I have no children to leave a property to, and nor are prices rising significantly as they once were.

But the broker crunches some numbers and I'm amazed when they come out significantly different from my previous investigations. It turns out that with the money I'm earning it will be easy to buy a small flat – especially when I discover how much deposit I can release from pensions I took out when I was a salesman and have never paid into since. My feeling that it's now or never is reinforced when almost immediately I view a beautiful, one-bedroom flat overlooking Swanage Bay. Why it's been on the market for over a year is beyond me, because everyone who visits it is stunned by the view. As am I, every morning.

I also know that if I finally buy somewhere there is a far greater chance that, at last, I'll stop moving around and finally settle in one place. Not before time.

The move into my new flat is unfortunately hampered, though, by a broken leg. While running a course in Brighton I'm walking away from my car in a multi-story when I hear an engine revving behind me. My initial thought is that some teenagers on a joy ride are intending to deliberately ram me, but everything happens so fast I don't even have time to turn round properly.

The car bumper hits my left leg just above the ankle and breaks both bones straight away. More worryingly I'm shot up into the air and, instead of coming back down on the bonnet or even roof as I might have expected, I land heavily on the concrete floor from a great height… smack on my lower back. I know from my racing days that I'm in massive shock – breathing very fast and shallow, shaking all over – and need proper assistance. But when several people try to call an ambulance they keep getting cut off. Eventually though one turns up and the medical staff are excellent, albeit that it takes some time to load me onto a stretcher. Although my leg is painful, they're more worried about my back, as am I. All I know is that I can wriggle the toes on both feet, so at least I'm not paralysed.

The poor woman who was driving the car is hysterical. She must have seen me rather late and, panicking, hit the accelerator instead of the brake. As they load me into the ambulance I try to reassure her that we all make mistakes. Then, after a wonderful session in the hospital's plastering section late that night – when they have to pull hard on my foot to make sure the bones don't start to set in the wrong place – I'm operated on the next day and they fit a metal rod from knee to ankle.

The advances in modern medicine since my racing days are quite fantastic. The scars where they operate are minimal, my leg doesn't need a plaster, and they tell me it's fully weight-bearing straight away – although of course mentally it takes time to build up to that. So I'm on crutches as the move happens, and have to elicit lots of help from friends and family. I am a pain in the neck too because I'm in proper project-manager mode, knowing that if people don't put things in the right place I won't be able to move them myself for some time.

Initially my whole lower abdomen feels somewhat numb, and I even worry that I've become impotent. But luckily that fear Is dispelled after a couple of weeks recuperation at my nephew Mike's flat – he is now married and he and his lovely wife Rachel are very good to me. Meanwhile the crutches are gone after about six weeks and, although my leg will never be perfect again, there's no real problem apart from the fact I can't kneel down very well. Then again my legs and hips were never particularly supple anyway. Moreover, just to prove that every cloud has a silver lining, the more-than-generous personal-injury payout reduces the term on my mortgage by about a third.

As far as work is concerned, just to spice life up a bit I've been on lots of foreign jaunts over the last few years. Previously I'd run occasional courses in far-flung locations such as Tripoli and Singapore, and closer to home Vienna, Lisbon, Madrid and Geneva. My Singapore trip even coincided with the F1 Grand Prix where, with tickets prohibitively expensive, I managed to march down the still-open road to the first corner as if I owned the place – just as my sisters had always taught me – then waited for several hours before watching the first few laps. Luckily as so often these were the only exciting ones anyway, because at that point the uniformed stewards finally rumbled that I didn't have a ticket and escorted me away.

But more recently I've taken several trips to Kiev – one while it's covered in deep snow when I've just got rid of my crutches, which makes me very nervous, particularly of falling on my back again. Even better QA has the contract for UN training and, because I like to see new parts of the world and it pays a little better, I've lately volunteered for several courses in Central Africa.

Liberia is an incredibly poor country, and on my first day I'm accosted by what turns out to be a fake policeman demanding money. South Sudan is marginally better, and since I'm there for two weeks I'm taken for several excellent late nights out by a local delegate with the inimitable name of Lovington. Addis Abbaba meanwhile is much larger, but though the people are very friendly I struggle to get into the social vibe of the place.

Yet perhaps my most fun trip of all has nothing to do with work. Instead it involves me acquiring a new set of teeth. I smoked heavily for years – as many as sixty roll-ups a day by the time I gave up in 2006 – and this tends to induce gum recession and disease, but it's masked because your gums don't bleed. By 2016 my teeth aren't looking too good, especially one of the main front ones – which is moving outwards at a rate of knots, presumably because of weakened bone in the upper jaw.

I visit the London branch of a highly recommended Hungarian clinic, but they tell me my gums are in real bad shape and need to be sorted before I have any cosmetic work done. So I find a London specialist who is the only one to offer a relatively new treatment using lasers, rather than gum surgery. I end up having around twenty-seven hours of same over several months and it costs me many thousands of pounds, but it's worth it – my gums are almost completely rescued.

As soon as possible after that I arrange my trip to Budapest where, for a very reasonable price compared to the UK, I will be having the six central teeth in each of my upper and lower jaws renewed with a combination of caps and bridges. Not only that but they'll do it all in one go, so I only need to take six days off work. It is a beautiful city, but I have little time to explore before my first appointment on a Monday afternoon. It is a good thing they didn't warn me that I'd be in the chair for five hours straight.

Although my dentist speaks hardly any English

it's a very professional setup, and he injects me thoroughly so that I feel no pain throughout. But the air is filled with the smell of burning enamel as he spends the first few hours filing my own teeth down to long, pointed stumps – at the end of which a cursory glance in the mirror reveals what appears to be one of Dracula's over-excitable cousins. Next he takes casts and has a temporary set of teeth made up, which I will wear over the next week to avoid frightening the local children.

In the interim I sample the nightlife and visit several of the infamous 'ruin bars', where dilapidated concrete buildings from the Soviet era have been turned into wonderfully eclectic drinking dens. In one the DJ is playing banging house tunes while scratched and flickering black-and-white films of motor racing from the early twentieth century are being projected onto the back wall. I am pretty sure I've died and gone to heaven.

On the Thursday afternoon I go back for the trial fitting of my new teeth, and find that the technician has worked a miracle. By thickening the one-piece crown over my two central upper teeth he's managed to ensure one doesn't stick out more than the other, and I have my 'Hollywood smile'. But my joy is short lived. When the dentist finishes, for some reason he decides not to glue the temporary bridges and caps at the bottom back in. I find this out when the bus brakes hard on the way back to the hotel... and I nearly swallow one. I am close to home though so decide not to go back. I figure I'll just have to be careful.

Which is fine, except for when I've had a few drinks. On the Friday night I'm in the gents at a bar chatting away to a chap when suddenly all three lower pieces – that's six teeth's worth – decide to fly out of my mouth onto the none-too-clean tiles. He actually screams and runs out shouting, 'That guy's teeth just fell out on the toilet floor!' Thanks buddy, I thought you were one of the good guys.

Anyway I retrieve them, give them a thorough clean and pop them back in. Not a disaster, I've been through worse. But then comes Saturday night. I am in a club dancing, and am both delighted and terrified to find myself surrounded by attractive local girls. I keep repeating to myself over and over again, 'Don't smile... don't smile... don't smile.' But then of course I pull a particularly energetic shape on the dance floor, or something, and all of a sudden... Pop! Out they come again.

So I'm scrabbling around on the floor trying to find them, and all the girls who've previously been smiling at me now think I'm some kind of pervert trying to look up their skirts – which is marginally better than them knowing what's actually going on. I find two out of the three pieces and decide to cut my losses. I spend the entirety of the following day trying not to look like a complete tramp and, while I've never looked forward to going to the dentist before, the following morning can't come soon enough.

But enough of high jinks. On a more serious note, where does all this leave us? In particular what happens if I use the principles of my new model of Supersoul Spirituality, as opposed to the more traditional model of Rational Spirituality – to analyse my own life? (By the way I think of the new framework as being entirely rational too, it's just that it needed a different name.) Perhaps this can shed useful light on how it all works?

So, first off, was it a special coincidence – or a 'synchronicity' somehow planned in advance – that I met Sarah... and for that matter Chris, Andy, Todd and all the other people who've had a major impact on the course of my life? Under the traditional model this was always how I looked at it, but under our new model things are rather different. I would argue that apparent synchronicities only represent the sophisticated underlying dynamics of how our *own* creation and attraction process crystallises into our experience during our life.

By that I mean that I did already have a vague interest in the alternative world of von Daniken et al even before I met Sarah, so I'd argue she came into my life as a response to that. The fact I had a strong urge to follow her was just the universe's way of telling me this would be a good idea if I wanted to pursue a side of life I'd already demonstrated an interest in.

Similarly, did Katherine and I have some sort of 'soul contract' whereby she would test me to my limits, as I originally believed? At the time this may have been a comforting thought that lessened the pain, but I now rather doubt it. Under our new model I think it's pretty clear that I manifested a perfect victim's partner who was often emotionally and physically unavailable due to other complications in her own life, and who quite understandably became less attached to me as I went downhill. We don't need to resort to any other explanation.

Related to all this, what of the traditional model's insistence that we have guides who 'know what is best for us' and try to keep us 'on our path'? This idea is not unrelated to that of 'surrendering to the flow' as discussed in the last chapter. The question is what path or flow – or more precisely *whose*? It can surely only be the flow of our own creation, both conscious and unconscious. What it surely *isn't* is some sort of plan formed in advance by other entities that somehow have a better idea of what would be best for us – whatever *best* might mean.

Remember that under the new model, because all lives are happening at the same time, the idea that we're 'growing' – by choosing, planning and facing different challenges as we progress from one life to another – is now out of the window. In particular I find the traditional model's suggestion, that supposed growth is often achieved only through suffering, isn't just a nonsense but can be actively harmful – it certainly was to me during my dark night.

So it seems to me now that, rather than us having any sort of advance plan, the complete opposite is true. Subject to our birth givens, as adults we have complete free will to direct our lives in any way we see fit, and to change that direction at any time. This means, as you'll recall, that our aim under the new model is to paint the best picture we can with our palette of birth givens – 'best' now meaning whatever we ourselves choose it to mean at any given time.

Second, then, who exactly are Big Bill and the other personalities I encountered in my regression sessions? I certainly don't now reject them as mere products of my imagination, nor for that matter all the other cases I examined closely in *The Big Book of the Soul* as strong evidence for past lives. That would be way too much of an illogical about-turn. Yes I'm definitely more aware now just how much we're capable of fabricating a convincing past-life narrative from information we already know, even to the extent of using different voices, accents and so on. But this doesn't explain the more evidential cases such as that of Big Bill, or the women in Peter Ramster's video.

Yet I don't have to see them as *past* lives for them to still have validity. What if instead they're what I refer to as 'resonant souls'? My suggestion is that these are other aspects of my supersoul with whom I have an especially close connection – for example, because of strongly shared traits or challenges, or because they act as contrasts. Their lives are continuing alongside mine, and we can even interact and learn from each other if we *choose*.

This also means that past-life therapy still has validity. In fact most therapists accept that it doesn't really matter whether the past lives experienced are real or not, not least because it's often easier for someone to process a trauma by experiencing something similar in a supposed past life rather than relive it in this, at least initially. But what must remain sacrosanct is that the prime responsibility for my own experience in this life lies with me – and no other entity, no matter how resonant, can exert a major influence unless I *choose* to believe they can or to let them.

Third, was my dark night of the soul self-created

or planned in advance? I would say it was a mixture of the two, but not because of any sort of formal life plan. Instead it's reasonable to suggest that my birth givens made a susceptibility to victimhood a reasonable probability. Why? Consider the fact that I was a sensitive and shy child, meaning that when my parents sent me to boarding school there was a fairly high probability of bullying, which is how it turned out until I found the strength to stick up for myself. I would suggest this experience set up a victim archetype within me that was then easily reactivated all those years later.

Nevertheless I could still have conquered my dark night far earlier if I'd been using our new model, had realised that all the elements of my victim experience were unconsciously self-created and self-perpetuating, and had consciously decided to change said experience. Not least by choosing to no longer be a victim, as I eventually did, except rather late.

But, let's face it, the question you *really* want the answer to is this: in what parts of my life as a creator god have I really screwed up? After all, that's what this book is supposed to be about. I may have cracked deliberate manifestation in some areas, such as having long-term work, strong finances, good housing and plenty of friends – and in all of these I've consciously used visualisation and other techniques to create the outcomes I desire. But there are definitely other areas where I've had significantly less success. Maybe some other authors gloss over their failures, but this was always intended to be a warts-and-all account of my life and creations – and I'm not going back on that now.

The first point to make is to refute those who insist, 'There can't be any screw ups. Everything that happens is just *perfect* because it gives us a chance to learn and grow.' Sorry, but I've come to the conclusion this is absolute, total, utter, traditionalist nonsense. Yes of course everything that happens adds to our supersoul's database of experience, and from that perspective there's no sense of 'good' or 'bad'.

But remember that, subject to our birth givens, we can manifest unlimited abundance in whatever areas we choose – and nor is there any necessity to suffer in order to grow. So as individual humans navigating our way through the Earth game, it goes without saying that we can attract some outcomes that are less desirable to us as individuals than others – screw-ups, in other words.

We have already seen a number of smaller examples of how I've obviously screwed *something* up. Just recently, for example, writing off my race car and breaking my leg both spring to mind as less-than-ideal experiences that I must have attracted into my life – even if in these two cases I'm completely unable to fathom the underlying dynamics of *how* I did it.

But of course there are also rather larger areas of my life where I've been screwing up for years. Indeed it's rather sad to report that arguably these are the only two that I *really* care about. They are my desire to find a truly loving, long-term partner, and to make a success of my writing and research. Indeed my attempts at conscious creation in these areas have been *so* disastrous for *so* long that I've pretty much given up on them. Not that that's an easy thing to do, but sometimes it can all get too much.

Some of you will say, 'There! I told you! The only areas you really care about are the ones where you're powerless to do anything. It's all poppycock!' Nor do I necessarily blame you. My Bristolian friend Gary once said to me, 'No wonder your books don't sell. If I wanted to know about creating my perfect life, I'd want to read a book by someone who was actually *good* at it!' And he had a point. But bear with me, because this is the whole crux of this book. We have all the analysis we need at our fingertips to explain my lack of success in these areas – without having to resort to pretending that conscious creation is a figment of our imagination, when in reality it remains a fundamental feature of our existence.

Think about it. You intensely desire an outcome in a particular area of your life. Quite often over a period of years you appear to manifest it, but each time it's only short lived. This has a number of effects. First, it tends to make you tighten up on your desire, and maybe want it *too* much. Second, each episode of failure gnaws away at you, reducing your inner belief. Although you theoretically know what you're capable of, in practical terms your inner voices of self doubt are having a field day.

This *doesn't* mean you turn into a victim, nor

does it mean you suddenly forsake the law of attraction as something that 'doesn't work'. You know and accept that your inner beliefs and so on are creating the undesirable outcomes – you just *also* accept that you're really struggling to turn the situation around. You can do all the inner work you like, but sometimes it appears that you just don't get to the root of the problem, or it just becomes too deeply ingrained.

Once an area of your life gets that bad, I liken it to a supertanker. You *can* turn it around. But it has such momentum that doing so will take a long time and consistent effort and belief. What is more, of course, any further failures during that time will tend to push it back towards its original course.

Since in these two key areas of my life I've been manifesting consistent failure for more than a decade, let's look at each a little more closely.

As far as partners are concerned, I have mentioned several as we've gone along, but no relationship has lasted more than around three years ever since I was in my twenties. I have never been married, and for much of the last decade I've been on my own. Some people in long-term relationships might envy that, but the truth for me is that I've often felt extremely lonely, especially with no children of my own. There is a danger of all that sounding like self-pity, but it's not, it's just a statement of the facts. Have I given up during this time? No. Anyone who knows me will confirm that after each disappointment I dust myself off and, maybe after a suitable period to heal and recentre, open myself up to love again.

Of course many people meet their partner through their work, but I'm always on the move, and in any case my delegates are under far too much pressure to be thinking of romance. This means I've not been averse to using internet dating on occasion, and I know this can work wonderfully for some people. But not, it seems, for me.

On one of my very first dates many years ago I turned up at Richmond station ready to meet the love of my life – I was new to it all then, and full of hope – but as I drove into the car park the only person I could see was definitely not the one in the pictures. Without wanting to be unkind, I could see from a distance that she was as wide as she was short, she was wearing nylon flairs and a quilted anorak, her hair hadn't been washed for some time, and the whole ensemble was capped off with bottle-top glasses.

Of course I hoped against hope that wasn't her, while knowing deep inside it was. I drove round the back of the car park to play for time, with my good angel on one shoulder saying, 'You've arranged to go out for lunch, you can't let her down,' while the bad angel was urging me to get the hell out of there. The former was just about winning as I edged round near to where she was and pulled up behind a parked van. It was at this point that said van decided to start reversing and, in my discombobulated state, I found myself frozen in time. Unable to find the horn or reverse gear I watched helplessly as, in slow motion, he backed into my front bumper. Just two minutes before my life had looked so much rosier.

On another occasion – and again I really don't mean to be unkind – I found that the quirky but attractive face in the pictures, which carried only a slight squint, was in fact adorning someone less than five feet tall with a significant hunch on her back. Of course looks are no reason not to get on with someone, but sadly neither of these women was particularly interesting either.

More recently, though, I've found myself attracting women on dating sites who seem to be incredibly judgmental. Don't get me wrong, of course I'm not the perfect man by any stretch, but when I see what most men get up to in relationships I reckon I at least deserve a shot. I am house-trained, reasonably tidy, can do my own washing and cooking, I don't slouch on the sofa endlessly watching football while scratching and rearranging my nether regions, nor do I play computer games at all hours of the day and night. I can also buy flowers, be kind and loving etc., etc., etc... but this isn't a dating advert.

Of course I'm perfectly aware that there must be wonderful women out there, some of them even on dating sites. But as far as the ones I've attracted are concerned – well I guess they've mirrored what must by now be multiple insecurities back to me by being judgmental and even downright unkind. Meanwhile my closest friends are genuinely perplexed that after all these years I've still never met 'the one'.

Recently it has got to the point where I've decided I have to let it all go. After yet another online dating disaster with a woman I never even got to meet I've just cried, 'Enough!' I have stopped including meeting the girl of my dreams in my daily affirmations, and finally accepted that I might never meet her. I acknowledge that, especially since I'm not prepared to compromise on love and just be with someone for the sake of it, I might have to face the rest of my life alone. In one sense that decision is extremely scary and uncomfortable. On the other hand it feels liberating, as if the pressure is off. It also means I'm having to fully and finally confront a fear I haven't wanted to face before.

Of course this release may be just what's needed for me to finally meet 'the one'. But I'm certainly not counting on it.

So what about the other supertanker – the one with my books on it? Well, again we've heard that during my dark night sales dwindled to almost zero, and that's where they've stayed ever since. So much so that some time back I decided to remove my earlier Rational

Spirituality publications from print. It simply wasn't worth the hassle of trying to keep accounts relating to miniscule sales of quite a few different books.

Nor has the situation changed since the publication of my whole new set of offerings under the banner of Supersoul Spirituality. When *Supersoul* and *The Power of You* came out I sent a number of copies to other authors, often those referenced heavily therein. But hardly a single one even acknowledged receipt. I did the same with organisers of conferences and talks, but got nowhere.

Again this might sound like self pity or, god forbid, as if my dreaded victim archetype is rearing his ugly head again. But he's not. These are just the facts. Nor am I leaving out any good news to exaggerate the situation. Apart from the very occasional bit of positive feedback, and Stephen and Margaret's being interested enough to try to persuade me to write this book, there isn't any.

I am aware that *Supersoul* is quite a heavy read, especially at the end, but *The Power of You* is much simpler. In fact long, long after it came out a number of good friends have told me what a wonderful and inspirational piece of work they think it is. One, Sandy, has herself written a groundbreaking book detailing the formally backed study she managed to instigate in a Birmingham hospital, showing spiritual healing having terrific results on patients with IBS. Even though our meeting on this occasion was a surprise, she was carrying *The Power of You* in her handbag and showed me all the pages covered in highlighting, insisting she reads a passage every morning to motivate herself.

This is of course wonderful to hear. But when you find out that in recent years each of my newer books – that is the two more formal ones and the two simpler ones – has sold a *maximum* of ten copies per year, you'll understand how desperately demoralising, indeed agonisingly painful, the situation is. As before, word of mouth just doesn't seem to be taking hold. Some people love to remind me of how many famous people's work was only recognised after their death, but I'm not exactly sure that makes me feel better.

Am I aware that I'm entirely responsible for creating this situation, just as I am with my romantic life? Yes, of course. This is all my doing at some level of my consciousness. So what is my attitude now? The one thing I know now is that whenever I gather up my strength to write a new book, I'm accepting that literally no one may read it apart from me. It has to be this way, otherwise the pain of dashed expectations becomes unbearable. That hasn't stopped me writing this one. Nor will it stop me completing *Afterlife* and its simpler, again controversially titled companion, *Death Should Be Fun!!*

I also know that just maybe this shift in attitude will be the one that frees everything up, so that one of these will be the book that finally gets people talking about and buying my work. But again am I banking on it? Decidedly not.

Supersoul Spirituality contains all sorts of theory, some of it more complex than others. But I hope by now you'll have realised that it has practical applications to our everyday lives too – and that I do attempt to practice what I preach.

Nowhere is this more true than with my awareness that I'm creating or at least attracting every aspect of my life, both good and bad.

When I say this to some friends they look at me as if I'm mad, and I know they're trying to be kind as well as truthful when they tell me they think I'm taking way too much responsibility for what they see as the continual *bad luck* that has befallen me with, for example, partners and books. But I can tell you unequivocally that, if I didn't have the belief that I'm responsible for all aspects of my experience to guide me, the series of disasters I've experienced in these two crucial areas of my life for so long would have defeated me long ago. I would have sunk back into victimhood and self-pity, and I'd either be a dribbling wreck or no longer even here.

The most important thing of all is I know I can't be creating the entirety of my experience *and* be a victim at the same time, because they're mutually exclusive. So I don't sink. What is more I have plenty of other areas of my life that are fine and fun, and for which I'm exceedingly grateful – even if it's to myself for creating them.

In a world that can be a bitch to navigate, so that even us gods screw up sometimes, I reckon that's got to be good enough.

the precepts and principles of Supersoul Spirituality

THE THREE PRECEPTS

1 Everything is Happening in the Now

Time is only a form of illusion that allows us humans to make sense of our experience of this plane. But fundamentally the past and future don't exist – there's only *now*. The implication is that it no longer makes sense to talk about past-life karma or next-life plans. Nevertheless it remains clear that each of us has a set of what I call 'birth givens', and that these vary widely – in terms not just of our sex but also of our main psychological and physical traits and propensities, and the socio-economic position and geographical location of our parents. So who chooses these?

2 Each of Us is a God in Our Own Right

The choice of our birth givens must fall to a level of our consciousness operating outside of space-time, whose aim is only to expand itself through different experiences in different worlds and realities via different forms. The 'supersoul' is a level of individuated consciousness repeatedly described by pioneering OOB explorers, whose encounters with such creative and wise entities lead them to think they're in the presence of a true divinity – until they come to realise this is just another aspect of themselves, and it's actually *who they really are*.

Supersouls are the very entities who create whole new universes to play in – or new simulations in a vast digital game. Yet we should be clear that there are myriad supersouls projecting aspects of themselves just into this version of the game called being human on Earth, so we're talking about something quite different from any concept of a universal Source consciousness.

The implication is that if only we understood just how powerful we really are, and that we've only temporarily taken on the form of human actors in a grand play, we might finally recognise that we're not limited and puny beings constantly buffeted by God's will, outrageous fortune and so on.

My definition of a supersoul therefore runs as follows:

> A supersoul is a grouping of hundreds, maybe thousands, of souls. Myriads of supersouls are projecting individual soul aspects of themselves into this and myriad other

realities, meaning they are very far from the ultimate consciousness. Yet to be fully connected to your supersoul is to have boundless wisdom and creative power, and as a full holographic representation of it you're already more divine than you can hope to conceive – divine enough, even, to nullify further speculation about what lies beyond.

3 The Law of Attraction Reigns Supreme

Experienced OOB explorers have come to realise that in higher planes their thoughts and emotions instantly translate into what they experience. The same principle underlies our earth reality. However here the constraints of space-time mean there's usually a time delay between thought and manifested result. Meanwhile the fact that ours is a 'consensus' or shared reality – in which our own thoughts and intentions are mingling and sometimes competing with those of our fellows around us – means the link between thought and manifested result is even more difficult to trace.

Couple this with the fact that our subconscious thoughts and beliefs are hugely powerful and often in conflict with our conscious desires, and you have the recipe for a hugely persuasive illusion where it *seems* that things are happening *to* us. But they're not. Instead everything each one of us experiences is, one way or another, created or attracted *by* us.

The implication is that the reality we're experiencing only acts as a mirror that projects our own thoughts and beliefs back to us. Of course this doesn't fully apply until we become adults and take on responsibility for ourselves, and it's also subject to any insurmountable limitations imposed by our birth givens.

THE TEN PRINCIPLES

1. We are multidimensional, expeditionary soul probes sent out by a supersoul consciousness possessing a wisdom and power of divine proportions. Myriad supersouls are involved in the simulation game we call 'human life on earth', which is just one of myriad different realities soul probes are sent into.

2. After death we continue to identify with the personality of the life we just left, so this and the 'soul' are the same consciousness.

3. Although we're still engaged in the growth of consciousness, we don't develop in a linear fashion as we move from one reincarnatory life to another. Instead the lives of all soul probes projected by the supersoul are happening at the same time – even if they're operating in different human eras – and they interact as a complex matrix. By logic alone this means the 'interlife' is only an *after*life, and possibly a *pre*life too.

4. 'My' many lives means nothing unless we're genuinely adopting our supersoul level of consciousness, which involves appreciating that we're far more powerful and multi-faceted than we normally recognise. Any experiences we have of 'past' or 'future' lives are most likely those of other 'resonant souls' from our supersoul with whom we have an especially close connection – for example because of strongly shared traits or challenges, or because they act as contrasts.

5. Each of us is fundamentally responsible for creating our own experience in each moment of now. We're not limited by 'past karma' from this life or a supposedly previous one unless we believe we are. Nor

will other resonant souls tend to be able to exert a strongly disruptive influence over us unless we believe they can and choose to let them.

6. Our supersoul chooses our 'birth givens', and these vary considerably. They include our own sex, our main psychological and physical traits and propensities – in terms of both challenges and strengths – and the socio-economic position and geographical location of our parents. On that basis we're here to 'paint the best picture we can with the palette we've been given'. Other than that any pre-birth planning of events in our adult lives, or 'soul contracts' with others, are probably kept to a minimum to give us maximum free will to direct our experience. It's also unlikely that most of us have a preplanned 'life purpose', because again this would tend to detract from our free will to follow whatever purpose we desire – and to change that purpose, should we so choose, at any time.

7. Angels and guides may well be other aspects of our own supersoul, and they won't tend to interfere with our experience on the basis

that they supposedly 'know best' and 'want to keep us on our path'. Usually therefore synchronicities will only represent the sophisticated underlying dynamics of how our *own* creation and attraction process crystallises into our experience of the physical.

8. Having said that, insights and guidance are always available if we *proactively* ask for them, or if we *attract* them to ourselves automatically by our conscious intentions and actions. Such guidance might come, for example, from wiser, non-incarnate aspects of our supersoul consciousness, or from other resonant souls who've overcome similar challenges. We can also provide guidance to them by overcoming our own challenges, if they're open to it.

9. On rare occasions we might make a new agreement with our supersoul, at a subconscious level, to take on a new challenge in our adult lives. But it's always best to take responsibility for any challenge by assuming you created or attracted it, or at least by knowing you control your reaction to it. Any tendency to ascribe

challenges to 'past' karma, life plans or soul contracts can lead to an abrogation of responsibility for what we're creating in the now, and detract from our extensive power to turn any situation around.

10. Under a matrix model *everything* can be seen as altruistic, because everything that each soul experiences is designed to add to the databanks of the supersoul consciousness. Any particularly challenging circumstances or birth givens can best be seen in the context of 'taking one for the team', and each of us can be characterised as a 'lead representative of team supersoul gaining experience at the coalface of space-time on behalf of the collective'.

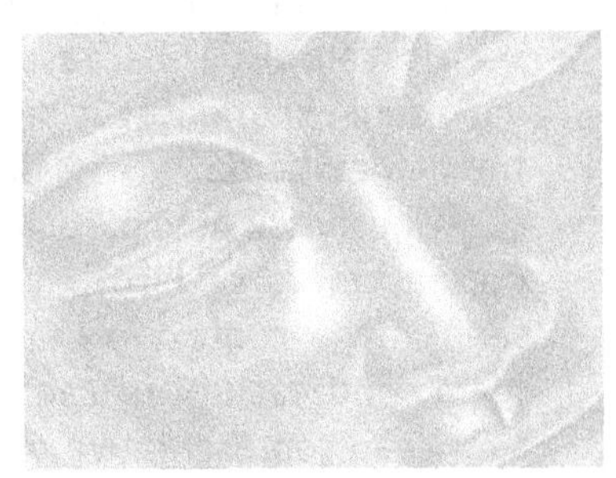

plates section

Father Syd winning the North West 200 on the 500cc works Norton in 1953, and (inset) in the paddock afterwards.

The Family before my arrival. (L to R) John, Pam, Syd, Beryl, Barry, Christine, Sheila.

On godfather Bob McIntyre's knee at my christening. He set the first 100mph lap at the TT in 1957

Keen on bikes from an early age.

With brother Barry, Aermacchi mounted at Snetterton in 1982. He won with me second.

On Syd's 422cc Aermacchi, winning the Classic Senior Race of the Year at Snetterton in 1983.

The podium at Monza in 1989 that I'd visualised the night before. Bill Swallow is on the left.

Against Bill again, Pre-TT Classic two weeks later. Leading but no longer on the bike.

350cc Formula 2 Yamaha
mounted, Brands Hatch, 1986

Up against the works AFN Carrera
4 in my 2.7 RS in the Porsche
Supercup, Snetterton, 1991.

With co-author Chris after our night time foray into the Sphinx enclosure in 1998.

The gorgeous mv Ullyses that I lived on from 2001 to 2003.

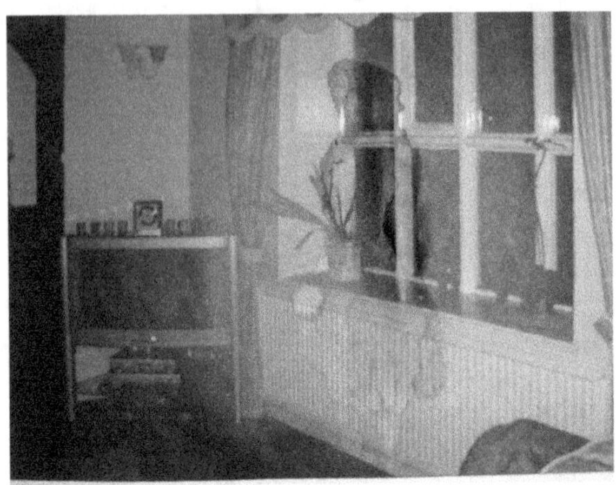

One of the faked 'ghost' pictures from 2006. Note the retrospectively obvious white line at the base where the photo was scanned.

That first view from the Purbeck Ridge at Nine Barrow Down, Christmas 2008.

One of the larger driftwood mirrors I created in my Westbourne flat in 2009.

Great friend Kenny and I prepare to leave for our Isle of Man trip on completely untested bikes in 2010. My Honda CB500 café racer on the left, his CB750 on the right.

With good friend and colleague Andy Tomlinson after graduating from his regression academy in 2011.

The original Love Bus, converted in 2011.

The cosy interior of the Love Bus.

The Honda CB750 café racer I built up in 2012.

The New Love Bus, converted from an ex-library bus in 2017.

The spacious interior of the New Love Bus.
Note the four-poster bed at the rear.

Sharing a joke with nephew
Michael at his wedding in 2017.

After my first race in twenty-two years.
MG ZR160, Donington Park, 2017.

Last but by no means least, my faithful companion through good times and bad, Bryan

the Supersoul Series

all published by Rational Spirituality Press
see *www.rspress.org* and *www.ianlawton.com*

RESEARCH BOOKS

[Volume 1] SUPERSOUL (2013) is the main reference book for Supersoul Spirituality, containing out-of-body and channelled evidence that each and every one of us is a holographic reflection of a supersoul that has power way beyond our wildest imaginings.

[Volume 2] THE POWER OF YOU (2014) compares modern channelled wisdom from a variety of well-known sources, all emphasising that each of us is consciously or unconsciously creating every aspect of our own reality, and that this is what the current consciousness shift is all about.

[Volume 3] AFTERLIFE (2019) is a state-of-the-art, clear, reliable guide to the afterlife based on the underlying consistencies in traditional channelled material and modern out-of-body research.

SIMPLE BOOKS

SH*T DOESN'T JUST HAPPEN!! (2016) introduces Supersoul Spirituality by explaining how and why we ourselves create or attract everything we experience in our adult lives... so that we are never victims of chance, God's will, our karma or our life plans.

WHAT JESUS WAS REALLY SAYING (2016) is a fundamental reinterpretation of the Christian message that uses excerpts from the Gospels to propose that, through his supposed miracles, Jesus was trying to show us that each of us is a creator god of the highest order and can manipulate the illusion we call reality at will.

THE GOD WHO SOMETIMES SCREWED UP (2018) charts the author's progression from motorcycle and car racer, to pyramid explorer and researcher of ancient civilisations, to spiritual philosopher... with analysis and examples of how he has created or manifested all the various aspects of his life, both good and bad.

DEATH SHOULD BE FUN!! (2019) is a light-hearted look at the afterlife, concentrating on the unlimited possibilities we have to create wondrous new experiences in the higher planes of consciousness… as long as we have a map of the territory, and we're aware that we're in control and that the sky's the limit.

IAN LAWTON was born in 1959. Formerly an accountant, sales exec, business and IT consultant and avid bike and car racer, in his mid-thirties he changed tack completely to become a writer-researcher specialising in ancient history and, more recently, spiritual philosophy. His first two books, *Giza: The Truth* and *Genesis Unveiled,* sold over 30,000 copies worldwide.

In his *Books of the Soul Series* he originated the ideas of Rational Spirituality and of the holographic soul. But since 2013 he has been developing the more radical worldview of Supersoul Spirituality in the *Supersoul Series*. A short film clip discussing the latter can be found at *www.ianlawton.com* and on YouTube.

www.ingramcontent.com/pod-product-compliance
Lightning Source LLC
LaVergne TN
LVHW010637110826
845149LV00014B/2860

* 9 7 8 0 9 9 2 8 1 6 3 4 6 *